UNEVEN LIES

The Heroic Story of African-Americans in Golf

American Golfer titles may be purchased for business or promotional use for special sales.
For information, please write to: The American Golfer, Inc., 200 Railroad Avenue,
Greenwich, Connecticut 06830.

The American Golfer and its logo, its name in scripted letters,
are trademarks of The American Golfer, Inc.

SECOND EDITION

ISBN 1-888531-36-3

Published by:
The American Golfer
200 Railroad Avenue
Greenwich, Connecticut 06830
203-862-9720 (Tel)
203-862-9724 (Fax)
imd@aol.com (E-mail)

Designed by:
GraphixWorks
51 Hemlock Trail
Trumbull, Connecticut 06611
203-377-3647 (Tel)

Film and Separations by:
Gateway Graphics
140 Water Street
Norwalk, Connecticut 06854
203-853-4929 (Tel)

ACKNOWLEDGEMENTS
Many thanks to Titleist for making this book possible;
to Craig Bowen for his dedication in seeing it through;
and to Dr. Calvin H. Sinnette for lighting the way.

Grateful acknowledgements to the PGA of America and the United States
Golf Association for helping set the record straight and to the following individuals:
Brett Avery, Linwood Barnes, Joe Louis Barrow Jr., Al Battle, Charles T. Bell Sr.,
Moses Brooks, Ralph Brown, Frank Carpenter, Carol Clarke, Tolona Coward, Martin Davis,
Edward Dendy, William (Bill) Dickey, Barbara Douglas, Herman DuBois, Harold Dunovant,
Jack Edgerton, Jolene Elbashere, Bitsy Farnsworth, Sheila Fender, Terry Galvin,
Billy Gardenheight, Glen Greenspan, Bruce Grundlock, Frank Hannigan,
Richard (Jelly) Hansberry, Ernestine Harper, Rose Harper-Elder, Chet Harrington,
Maggie Hathaway, Dr. Marvin P. Hawkins, Gary Holmes, Isabella Holmes, Norris Horton,
Keith Jarrett, Sam Jefferson, Walter King, Boyce Layton Sr., Dr. Lawrence Londino,
Elrado Long, Julius Mason, Warren E. Massenburg, Frank Matthews, Terry McSweeney,
Phyllis G. Meekins, Charles (Eddie) Miller, Porter Pernell, Judy Rankin, Lisa Richards,
Mary Rung, Paul Runyan, Geoff Russell, Dr. Jeffrey Sammons, Roger Schiffman,
Paul Shannon, Lisa Vannais Shultz, Charlie Sifford, Dr. George Simkins Jr., Louise Simpson,
Craig Smith, Thomas (Smitty) Smith, Winifred Stanford, Henry Stone, Leticia Swift,
Timothy Thomas, George Henry Wallace, Peggy White, Tiger Woods, Eric Yeager.

Dedicated to those souls
who gave of themselves and their talent
to help level the lie in American golf.

To Kevin,

Best wishes and
enjoy the Story !!!

Yours in golf,

G. B. Bone

UNEVEN LIES

The Heroic Story of African-Americans in Golf

by Pete McDaniel

Edited by Geoff Russell and Martin Davis

Research by Craig Bowen

The American Golfer, Inc. • 200 Railroad Avenue • Greenwich, Connecticut 06830
tel 203-862-9720 • fax 203-862-9724 • e-mail imd@aol.com

TABLE OF CONTENTS

DETERMINATION AND GRIT

BY TIGER WOODS

"I must admit, the first time I drove down Magnolia Lane I was not thinking about Bobby Jones or all the Masters stood for. I was thinking about all the great African-American players who never got a chance to play there."

I am a product of two parents who came from different backgrounds but possess the same love for all humanity. Mom and Pop are my anchors through my trials, which have been many during my short life. They have always been instrumental in my educational process and for that I will be forever grateful. So much of who I am is because of them and the life lessons they espoused. They instructed me to dream big, set goals and strive with all my might to reach them, and, most of all, respect and appreciate people with diverse backgrounds and cultures, for I am no better or worse than anyone. They also taught me that in order to get a clear picture of where I want to go, I should know where I've been and something about those who were there even before me.

Golf has afforded me a stage for free expression. That freedom, however, was a gift paid for by many determined people who endured all kinds of indignities just to be able to play the game. I and every person of color who enjoys this great game can do so because of their determination and grit. I'm reminded of that every time I tee it up. I know where I've been.

Racism and segregation are not foreigners in America. As a minority, I have seen them face-to-face. When my Mom was late in her pregnancy with me, someone in our mostly white neighborhood in Cypress, Calif., hurled an orange through our kitchen window. Some of our neighbors had protested our arrival there by pelting our house with various fruits. Thankfully, Mom was not hurt and was able to carry me to term. The perpetrators were later discovered and dealt with, but it had set a tone of intolerance even before I was born.

Being the only minority in school, quite naturally I was a little nervous that first day when Mom took me to kindergarten. I never thought, however, that some of the older kids would tie me to a tree in the schoolyard and taunt me. I didn't understand it then. How could I?

I was a little better prepared for being run off the Navy Golf Course—which happened many times during my formative years—and the curious stares my parents and I got when I started playing tournament golf. By then, I knew I was different and that some people had a hard time accepting that difference. By then, Mom had shared with me how native Thais had always been looked down upon by those of Chinese descent. Pop had taught me how to recognize the look and, more importantly, how not to respond.

The pioneers who opened up the game for all of us had many of the same experiences. From John Shippen to Joe Louis, Bill Spiller, Ted Rhodes and Charlie Sifford and to Lee Elder, they all encountered the steamy glare of intolerance. Most of them understood that sometimes the best way to initiate change is to hold your peace. Confrontation only impedes progress and makes it more difficult for those who follow. Jackie Robinson understood that perfectly. He was one of my Dad's baseball idols, along with Roy Campanella and Willie Mays. Pop's baseball roots go back to Kansas where he grew up. He went to Kansas State on a scholarship and was the first African-American baseball player in the Big Eight Conference. That was in the '40s and '50s. He met a lot of the Negro League players during their barnstorming. The influence of these guys made it possible for him to keep going in a sport he loved. He helped me draw the historical connection between baseball and golf. I also did some investigating of my own in my sport to understand how the PGA Tour came to be a place where anyone could play, because that wasn't always the case. I know where I've been.

> "The pioneers who opened up the game for all of us had many of the same experiences ... they all encountered the steamy glare of intolerance."
> — Tiger Woods

In the spring of 1995, I went to receive an honor at a little 9-hole course in Indianapolis called Douglass Park. I knew from my research that Spiller, Sifford and Rhodes played there in the old days when the United Golfers Association tour was the only place they could compete. As I looked out over the tiny course, I could envision them in competition. A month later, I played in the Masters for the first time as U.S. Amateur champion. I have been asked many times how it feels to drive down Magnolia Lane at Augusta National. I have a great deal of reverence for Masters tradition, especially since my victory in 1997, but I must admit, the first time I drove down Magnolia Lane I was not thinking about Bobby Jones or all the Masters stood for. I was thinking about all the great African-American players who never got a chance to play there. That I was able to win there, I believe, brought a little bit of vindication for them. I know where I've been.

At the same time, I understand we cannot dwell in the past. We must move on and accept new challenges. I believe that I'm in a unique position, with my linear heritage, to actually touch more lives than any of the pioneers. My Asian heritage is one of the reasons I play around the world. I want to share this great game with everybody, just as it was shared with me. I also want to make golf look like America. All cultures are congregated here and that's how I'd like to make the game, so that long after I've holed my last shot, people will know that I was here.

AFRICAN-AMERICANS AND AMERICA'S GAME OF GOLF

by Pete McDaniel

Some wounds never heal. We wear the scars from others like a red badge of courage, a harsh reminder of an incident or an exclamation point on our personal timeline that sometimes sears our very soul.

The sun was fading behind the Blue Ridge Mountains as I pedaled my 3-speed bike homeward against light traffic on Mills Gap Road. The cool breeze brushed against my sweat-stained face and my knobby legs battled the incline. Every hundred yards or so I would feel for the small bulge in my pocket—six crumpled dollar bills, the caddie fee I had earned that afternoon for a double loop at Biltmore Forest Country Club. I was ever so careful when it came to sweat money. My father worked as a dish washer at a private boarding school. Mama worked in the laundry there and put in overtime as a domestic. Our family ate well, dressed even better and had a new car every four years around income tax time, but there was no discretionary cookie jar for allowances. Like most of the other young people in our neighborhood, when we were old enough to understand peer pressure, my siblings and I found odd jobs for financial independence and that new pair of Chuck Taylors—the tennis shoes of choice at that time.

My main gig was caddieing. I had other sidelines, like mowing lawns and baling hay. I even picked beans a couple of times. But the day my older brother returned from Biltmore Forest with a few shag balls and some folding money, all other enterprises suddenly lost their appeal. The club was one of the last bastions of southern aristocracy in Western North Carolina, a private playground for old-money families and eccentric millionaires. The course, a Donald Ross design constructed in 1922, was the site of several post-war PGA Tour events. After much pleading, I was allowed to tag along. I was only 11 and small for my age. The caddiemaster was a family friend and vowed to look after me. Little did he know what a big job he had consented to undertake.

On this day, my mood could not have been better. I didn't even mind the long, tedious bike ride home. I had more money than I left with and that would make Mama

*Mama with her school play stars (left to right) **Randy, Anthony (Pete)** and **Ellen**.*

proud. I lived to make Mama proud.

The pain from the blow to my back raced along my spine from neck to buttocks. The force from the blow knocked me into a briar patch. The handlebars pressed into my chest as I lay there in shock. I wheeled my head around just in time to get a good look at who and what had hit me. In the bed of a pickup truck, grinning, stood a freckle-faced, carrot-top teenager holding what appeared to be a slab of tire rubber. His companions—a driver and passenger—roared in laughter, oblivious to the oncoming traffic. Blood trickled down my face but my eyes remained dry. For a long time, their twisted faces and guttural jocularity would wake me from a sound sleep. Forgiveness did not come easy for me, but neither did quitting. A social climate hotter than Mama's chili could not quash my determination to be part of a world whose welcome mat had reservations.

> From the moment my brother and I jumped out of the family Chevy at the caddie lot, I felt a communal closeness to even the most grizzled loopers.

From the moment my brother and I jumped out of the family Chevy at the caddie lot, I felt a communal closeness to even the most grizzled loopers. The lot, enclosed by a chain-linked fence, was my home away from home. And the other caddies quickly became my extended family. There was always a basketball or ping-pong game going on. Scraped knees and knuckles were our proud war wounds from competition and conflict. But mostly, we played the waiting game. In those days, the caddiemaster would telephone his subordinate at the lot to request caddies. The caddie supervisor would in turn send those fortunate enough to be in his favor up the hill to the clubhouse, where the caddiemaster would assign them players. We referred to getting a loop as "getting out." It paid to be connected, obedient and politically correct. Those who weren't would find themselves blacklisted and loop-less.

I was too small to carry a regular-size bag, so the caddiemaster gave me and the other mites a job that required minimal lifting. We were shag boys, the lowest caddies by pecking order, but I, for one, was proud just to be earning ice cream money. Besides, I always attacked a job with fervor and planned to be the best shag boy there. Before long, I grew strong enough to carry a small bag nine holes. A couple years later, I stalked the hilly BFCC layout with a regular-size bag on each shoulder. I was a full-fledged, Class-A caddie, but my education extended far beyond that field of dreams. I quickly learned there was power behind the Sansabelts and hard-collared shirts. Securing some of it, however, could prove as tricky as a three-foot slider.

Caddies weren't allowed in the clubhouse, but I could envision the blue-hairs engrossed in a game of bridge and the suits gathered in the bar damning the politicians. I knew for sure the only faces like mine in that clubhouse were either mixing whiskey sours or tossing shrimp salad. The kind of people who were members of Biltmore Forest didn't mingle with the kind of people who worked there, except in a service relationship. The service people knew their place. We carried golf bags, cleaned mansions and babysat pampered progeny. When nightfall came, only the club's employees and domestics could be caught in the Forest. All others suffered the consequences of trespassing.

> My passion for the game grew as a caddie and player. On our days off, my friends and I could be found at the local municipal course at dawn.

Our family heritage was as much a part of the Forest as the rhododendrons and huge evergreens. My maternal great-grandmother owned most of the land that eventually became Biltmore Forest, N.C. She sold it to the Vanderbilts for a pittance. George Vanderbilt's palatial estate was the Forest's crowned jewel and a tourist attraction. Haughtiness pervaded the golf club, but not all members were swept along in its current. Some had an almost familial relationship with the clubhouse employees and the caddies. One of them, an elderly gentleman with a thick, gray mustache, whom I caddied for several times, noticed my interest in the game. One day after his round, he gave me four wooden-shafted golf clubs. "See if you can't find something constructive to do with these," he snorted. I learned how to play the game beating golf balls in a cow pasture with those clubs. Later, I bought a starter's set at a discount store and completed it a club at a time as finances allowed.

My passion for the game grew as a caddie and player. On our days off, my friends and I could be found at the local municipal course at dawn. We played until dark or until the ranger ran us off. Some of the ex-caddies were accomplished players despite homemade swings and substandard equipment. They didn't play for club championship trophies nor were they allowed to eat in the dining room, but they comported themselves with the same kind of decorum and etiquette as frequent BFCC guests Dr. Billy Graham, the world famous evangelist who lived nearby in Montreat, and Jess Sweetser, who won the U.S. Amateur in 1922. Some of them were world champion yarn spinners. Others told the story of their predecessors in

The clubhouse at **Biltmore Forest Country Club**, *where the author caddied as a youth.*

the game like a country preacher reciting scriptures from the Bible. It was from some of the old-timers at the muny that I learned about early African-American heroes of the game, Charlie Sifford, Teddy Rhodes, Bill Spiller and a hometown favorite named John Brooks Dendy, a three-time winner of the United Golfers Association Negro National Open. But it was not until I witnessed for myself golf played at another level by people of color that I realized—and appreciated—our connection to the game's umbilical cord in this country.

Even in black and white, before technicolor, it was impossible to overlook golf's color line. Inequity shouted over the hushed tones. My awakening came during the Skyview Open, for years one of the main stops on the North American Golfers Association Tour. The old-timers had regaled us with stories about Lee Elder and his domination of the Skyview. Elder had won the event a number of times before finally making it to the PGA Tour. His ascension was as close to the Rev. Martin Luther King's proverbial mountaintop as a former caddie could hope to get. There were others, such as Jim Dent, Jim Thorpe, Charlie Owens and James Black, who aspired to follow Elder's footsteps, just as he had followed Sifford's. And there were still others who had major-league dreams and minor-league games. They all played the Skyview.

I watched Dent launch missiles from the black clay tee boxes and Thorpe throw darts at sandy greens, but neither of them had Black's complete game. A Charlotte, N.C., native, Black could pull the string with a wedge, turn a 4-wood into a 5-iron and call his shots with the skill of a psychic.

Despite the prediction of a college professor, I became the sports editor of the Hendersonville (N.C.) Times-News.

He won the Skyview three consecutive years, the last two with me on the bag. Like many of his peers who forever traveled golf's back roads, Black lived hard and loose. His biggest obstacle might have been himself as much as close-fisted authority's fear of his natural ability. Ultimately, the inner demons were too much for my hero to overcome.

Meanwhile, I pursued my own dreams, in the classrooms instead of the fairways. But my abilities as one who aspired to be the next great American writer were so limited, according to a bespectacled English professor at the University of North Carolina at Asheville, that the odds were heavily stacked against my getting a job in journalism. "You will never be a writer," he chided. His prediction of failure only fueled my determination. I graduated on a Saturday afternoon in May of 1974—the first in my family to earn a college diploma—and received a telephone call from the editor of my hometown newspaper the following Monday. The next week my Afro hairstyle and I began a journey from the obituary pages of the *Asheville Times* to the cover of *Golf Digest* magazine, with several detours in between. The only constants in my life besides strong family ties were two infatuations— golf and writing. I was much better at the latter, although there was a stretch in my 20s when I sported a solid, single-digit handicap.

Covering the Ryder Cup at Valdarama in 1997, the author took a day trip to Morocco. Here I leave the Casbah.

As sports editor of *The New York Times*-owned Hendersonville (N.C.) daily through the '80s and into the '90s, the doors swung open at all types of golf clubs, even a few that had never allowed a black man on the first tee box. I played in pro-ams and invitationals around the Southeast, usually at minimal out-of-pocket expense, and was generally welcomed with a warmth I never received at home. I dined with the mayor, took grip-and-grin photos with other civic leaders and covered tournaments at the Hendersonville Country Club, but not once in 14 years was I invited to play there. The stench from some attitudes in the New South rose from just beneath the surface where the dirt was barely disturbed.

In the fall of 1993, I arrived in Trumbull, Conn., to join the staff of *Golf World*, the sister magazine of *Golf Digest*, with a load of small-town newspaper experience and some golf knowledge but little exposure to the world of big-time. Except for covering the '93 Masters, where mine was the only black face among the hundreds of reporters in the media center, and Lee Janzen's victory at Baltusrol in the U.S. Open that year, my major championship coverage had been limited to the couch in my living room. My title was senior writer, but might as well have been special project, like the basketball giant drafted for his raw potential rather than his proven ability. I was the first African-American staffer in *Golf World's* 46-year history, a symbol of "diversity," a '90s catch phrase that fell pleasingly from the lips of corporate heads with much more ease than implementation.

As such the pressure of performance was immediate but, by the grace of God, not insurmountable. My editors and fellow staffers, a collection of well-educated, open-minded professionals, greeted me in the spirit of patience and with outstretched hands. The magazine's reward, in my opinion, was a different perspective on issues concerning a game growing in popularity and, more importantly, its acceptance of minorities. My learning curve began with the Ladies Professional Golf Association and televised golf, which I covered for two years, and extended to almost every major amateur championship between Niagara Falls, N.Y. (home of the Porter Cup), and Killarney, Ireland (site of the 1996 Curtis Cup). By the time I left *Golf World* for *Golf Digest* in July of 1997, I had become an accomplished golf writer and chronicler of Tiger Woods' phenomenal career. I tracked Tiger from Stanford University to Bangkok, Thailand. I had also seen Andy Walker play an integral role in Pepperdine's surprising NCAA Division I championship, becoming the sport's second African-American member of a national championship team. I had also co-authored Earl Woods' bestselling book, *Training A Tiger*. My family circle grew to include the Woodses and anyone else I may have positively affected by word or deed. So immensely blessed am I that it is incumbent upon me to give back a portion of what has been given me.

One of the more poignant memories from my travels, though, has nothing to do with gratuity and everything to do with diminishing returns. In 1993, I was covering the PaineWebber Invitational, a Senior PGA Tour event in Charlotte hosted by Arnold Palmer, when I spotted a familiar face outside the yellow ropes at the practice range. His waistline was more round than I remembered and there was a sprinkle of gray in his close-cropped hair, but otherwise the years had been kind to James Black. We spent a few minutes getting reacquainted, during which he admitted his golfing skills were a mere shadow of their former greatness. But he believed he could still play. He said he was there as a spectator instead of a participant because he had been denied a sponsor's exemption by the tournament. I went on to cover the tourna-

Following Tiger.

ment that week, culminating with my story three days later chronicling Mike Hill's win. But for the rest of my stay in Charlotte, I couldn't get the memory of my visit with Black out of my head. He remains, in my opinion, the best player no one ever knew.

Forgiveness comes much easier for me now, although I have found that many other people of color in this game lie restless from the pain of a dark past. The souls of African-American golf pioneers cry for someone to tell their story. It's time America listened. It's a wonderful story.

CHAPTER 1

OF GREEN JACKETS AND GHOSTS

"To have a person I admire, a pioneer, take his time to come out and support me was unbelievable. That's when pride and joy just swelled up inside of me." —Tiger Woods, on Lee Elder's final-round visit at the 1997 Masters.

S o fleeting are moments of historical resonance that they require uncompromised attention. Earl Woods had said so many times. Whether he had read it somewhere as a result of his voracious appetite for literary soul food or come by it through osmosis during myriad life experiences is of little significance. The father of the world's most famous African-American golfer could pull it from his bag of mantras as easily as his son would flash that infectious smile. That's why it was particularly painful to watch Earl house-ridden on this splendid spring Sunday morning in Augusta, Ga., a day when his son, Tiger, would emerge from golf's looking glass with the ghosts of the game's past and the hopes of its future in tow.

Augusta National Golf Club was an ironic battleground for the game's emancipation. Tiger knew its history, that an African-American hadn't played in the Masters during the first 40 years of its existence. The azaleas and dogwoods in full bloom made nice beauty shots for network TV but they could not mask the plantation atmosphere inside the club's gates. Although it has been argued that the late Clifford Roberts, as one of the founders of the club, had the power to change the qualification for invitation so that an African-American could have been invited to play in the Masters, he never did so, opting to stick by the established criteria. In the face of growing criticism from liberal politicians and civil rights leaders during the late 1950s, Roberts, according to Charlie Sifford's autobiography, *Just Let Me Play*, once vowed that as long as he lived there would be nothing at the Masters except black caddies and white players. Although it has been disputed whether Roberts ever said this, the era ended in 1975, as Roberts himself welcomed the Masters' first African-American invitee, Lee Elder.

The clubhouse at the Augusta National Golf Club.

Tiger Woods en route to victory in the 1997 Masters.

Fifteen years later, the club accepted television executive Ron Townsend as its first black member.

Even with the possibility of a good showing by Tiger, Masters week was no more than of minor interest to most African-Americans. The only Sunday celebration they anticipated was the 50th anniversary of Jackie Robinson's breakthrough in major league baseball. Earl, a former college baseball player himself, fully understood the significance of his son's impending triumph and its connection with Robinson's defining moment.

> From the time Tiger was old enough to comprehend man's inhumanity to other men, Earl schooled him on his predecessors in the game.

That's part of the reason he was convinced that Tiger's ultimate purpose in golf transcended sport and that his mission was preordained by fate. However, this Sunday morning Earl wasn't wasting his breath praising his son. A recent near-death experience had taught him the value of conserving oxygen.

Earl slumped onto the sofa in the living room of the rented house that served as Team Tiger's digs during its stay in Augusta. His usually animated face looked tired. His movements were like watching a slow-motion instant replay on a sports highlight show. Several weeks had passed since a second heart bypass surgery and the 65-year-old former Green Beret wasn't recovering as speedily as he had hoped. A couple of setbacks had further delayed his rehabilitation.

"I still have a little shortness of breath and I tire easily," Earl said. "I feel like I've been run over by a truck."

He looked it, too. But Earl also wore a placid demeanor. A cool customer anyway, he was especially tranquil considering the circumstances. His son held a nine-stroke lead going into the final round of arguably the most prestigious golf tournament in the world and Earl appeared disinterested in Tiger's impending coronation as the game's latest, and perhaps most important, socially significant conqueror. Nothing could be further from the truth, though. Earl lamented not being physically able to watch Tiger play in person. He had always been there for his son's defining moments. He walked in the shadows as Tiger won six consecutive United States Golf Association

Bill Frakes/Sports Illustrated

Earl Woods, who raised his son to become a golf champion.

championships—three U.S. Juniors and an unprecedented three U.S. Amateurs—in the process becoming the first African-American to win either event. It would be unusual to not see Earl in Tiger's gallery.

Despite Earl's infirmity, Tiger would not have to make his most significant walk alone. His mother, Kultida, had always been there, too. She had trekked up and down Augusta National's hills all week. While in Bangkok earlier that year, 'Tida' visited a Buddhist temple where a monk revealed Tiger's fate. "He said my son will win Masters," Tida said proudly to a friend. Not that Earl is a man lacking in faith, but his calmness had less to do with the monk's forecast than a close encounter with a prowling Tiger the night before.

Earl and Tiger have always been "best friends."

Every evening that week, Tiger had distracted himself with marathon table tennis games. It was his way of winding down, "chilling out" as he put it. The competition was a sleeping tonic, an ineffective one this evening because restlessness drove him from the bed and into the cool, night air. Thoughts of the importance of his date with history the next day and of those who were denied an opportunity to make their mark on the game flooded his mind. From the time Tiger was old enough to comprehend man's inhumanity to other men, Earl schooled him on his predecessors in the game. Men such as Teddy Rhodes, Bill Spiller and Charlie Sifford, who would become Tiger's adopted godfather; men who knocked on doors only to have them slammed shut in their faces. Tiger not only carried the weight of his own expectations onto the world stage, he had the ghosts of golf's past in a crowded balcony cheering him on. The specter of it all both warmed and chilled him. On

Tiger at Augusta in 1997.

his way back to his room, Tiger spotted a light under Earl's door. He sat and chatted with his father for a short while. Earl always knew what to say. He also knew when no words were necessary. At peace with himself and his mission, Tiger went back to bed. Tomorrow would take care of itself.

Earl resigned himself to watching most of the final round on television. However, he planned to be waiting for Tiger somewhere near the 18th green when Tiger finished his historic stroll through Augusta National's elegant pine trees. Nothing could keep him away.

> Buoyed by Elder and other well-wishers, Tiger continued to march through Georgia like Jackie Robinson in golf shoes.

Lee Elder had a similar mind as he roamed the course in obscurity as a spectator. Earlier in the week, he had left a card of encouragement on Tiger's locker. As the latter walked to the first tee on Sunday, Elder emerged from the crowd and offered one last verbal assist. "Good luck," Elder said, his round face glowing.

Amateur **Tiger Woods** on the practice tee at Augusta as his father watches.

"I knew exactly what he meant," Tiger would say later. "That to me was one of the biggest highlights of the entire week. To have a person I admire, a pioneer take his time to come out and support me, was unbelievable. That's when pride and joy just swelled up inside of me."

Buoyed by Elder and other well-wishers, Tiger continued to march through Georgia like Jackie Robinson in golf shoes. He air-punched out more recycled misconceptions in four days than any statesman could in four lifetimes. Bursting with pride, Augusta National's black employees gathered around televisions in the clubhouse and caddie quarters. This felt good.

Apart from the colorful splendor of the week, the black-and-white facts overshadow the warm and fuzzies of Tiger's 12-shot postscript. He became the Masters' first minority champion and the game's youngest major champ at 21 years, three months and two weeks. His 18-under-par 270 total eclipsed by one the Masters record set by Jack Nicklaus in 1965 and tied by Raymond Floyd 11 years later. In all, Tiger set 20 Masters records and tied six others.

Just like he planned, an energized Earl met Tida at the course and they awaited their

Tiger with his mother, **Tida**, and father, **Earl**.

son's finish. After holing the record-setting putt, Tiger fell into Earl's arms. The world watched as tears of joy and relief flowed.

After rounds of interviews with the world's golfing press, both print and electronic, Woods retired to the Augusta National clubhouse to have the champion's customary dinner with the club chairman—and, in so doing, broke the club's (and the game's) final color barrier.

Tiger and *Earl* share an emotional embrace at the end of the historic 1997 Masters.

Later, a few friends and family gathered in celebration back at the house. In the revelry, someone noticed the guest of honor's absence. Tiger had retired for the evening. There, asleep in his room, lay the new champion clutching the green jacket awarded all Masters winners since Sam Snead in 1949. The ghosts were finally put to bed, too.

The Masters
Augusta National Golf Club, Augusta, Georgia
April 10–13, 1997

Finish	Entrant	Scores		Purse
1	Tiger Woods	70 – 66 – 65 – 69	270	$486,000
2	Tom Kite	77 – 69 – 66 – 70	282	291,600
3	Tommy Tolles	72 – 72 – 72 – 67	283	183,600
4	Tom Watson	75 – 68 – 69 – 72	284	129,600
5	Costantino Rocca	71 – 69 – 70 – 75	285	102,600
5	Paul Stankowski	68 – 74 – 69 – 74	285	102,600
7	Fred Couples	72 – 69 – 73 – 72	286	78,570
7	Bernhard Langer	72 – 72 – 74 – 68	286	78,570
7	Justin Leonard	76 – 69 – 71 – 70	286	78,570
7	Davis Love III	72 – 71 – 72 – 71	286	78,570
7	Jeff Sluman	74 – 67 – 72 – 73	286	78,570
12	Steve Elkington	76 – 72 – 72 – 67	287	52,920
12	Per-Ulrik Johansson	72 – 73 – 73 – 69	287	52,920
12	Tom Lehman	73 – 76 – 69 – 69	287	52,920
12	José Maria Olazábal	71 – 70 – 74 – 72	287	52,920
12	Willie Wood	72 – 76 – 71 – 68	287	52,920

CHAPTER 2

ON THE FRONTLINES: THE FIRST WAVE

"It sure would have been something to win that day."
—*African-American golfer John Shippen, who shared the lead after the first round of the U.S. Open in 1896.*

Like the unknown soldier, many African-Americans who contributed to the growth of the game in this country remain buried in history's tomb. Some, such as John Shippen, shook the game's foundation just by being where they were not welcome and refused to be ignored. Others, such as Joseph Bartholomew, one of America's first home-grown golf course architects, and Dr. George F. Grant, father of the wooden golf tee, quietly affected the game through invention and vision. The fact that their place in history may never be adequately acknowledged does not diminish their importance or lessen their stature in the game. They were heroes and role models in their own right. Each of them is a profile in courage, perseverance and dogged determination. Their muted voices speak clearly from the grave. This is their story.

Exclusionary and segregated, the games Americans play and their playgrounds historically have been either the personal property of society's self-appointed upper class or the pride of its much larger lower class. Even the game of golf, a pastime originated by Scottish and Irish peasants for their pleasure, quickly became tainted by American attitudes when it made its way across the Atlantic to these shores in the late 18th century. Transformed into a sporting contest for bluebloods and high brows, golf had little room for commoners and was closed altogether to people of color and certain religious preferences. That's why it is particularly ironic that the first national exposure of an African-American in the game occurred during a competition categorized as an "Open".

Born out of conflict in 1894 and charged with governing the game, establishing rules and conducting various competitions in this country, the United States Golf Association welcomed the world's top players to Shinnecock Hills Golf Club in July 1896 for the second U.S. Open Championship. Serious golf had just begun to take root here. The association's premier event, the U.S. Amateur, had been completed days earlier at Shinnecock Hills, a links-style course constructed on property adjoining the Shinnecock Indian reservation in Southhampton, N.Y., on Long

Dr. George Grant, inventor of the golf tee.

John Shippen and the Shady Rest Country Club (inset).

Island. Many of the participants in the Amateur, won by H.J. Whigham of Scotland, decided to compete in the Open, at the time relegated to stepsister status to the more prestigious Amateur. Most of the 35 entrants were foreign-born whites. Two—Oscar Bunn and John Matthew Shippen Jr.—were natives, Bunn an American Indian and Shippen an African-American. Their presence in the field tested American athletic independence and, more importantly, the tenets upon which this country was founded a century earlier.

> ... at the age of 16, with the encouragement of many of the club's members, Shippen, along with Bunn, entered the United States Open Championship.

Shippen's road to Shinnecock began in the nation's capital. He was born in 1879 in Washington, D.C., one of nine children of a Presbyterian pastor. Nine years later, his father was sent by the church to minister at the Shinnecock reservation.

John quickly adapted to reservation life. His slight build belied an athleticism that enabled him to excel at most boyhood games and he became quite a sportsman. He knew nothing of golf, however, until 1891 when Scotsman Willie Dunn arrived in Southhampton to supervise construction of Shinnecock Hills. In need of laborers, Dunn raided the reservation. Shippen and Bunn were among the young workers who helped clear the land and construct the course intended to replicate British links layouts. Dunn also trained the pair and other young tribesmen as caddies. As the club's first professional, he shared his knowledge of the game with young John, who soon became a better player than any of the club's members and was elevated to the position of assistant to the professional. Shippen would rise early and report to the club for his various duties, including giving lessons and repairing clubs. Often, he served as starter and scorekeeper for club tournaments.

*Scotsman **Willie Dunn** supervised construction of the original Shinnecock Hills golf course and became the first head professional. John Shippen became his assistant.*

Shinnecock Hills Golf Club.

Jules Alexander

As his proficiency grew, so did his love for the game. He could not ignore the siren's song and Shinnecock became Shippen's road to opportunity. So at the age of 16, with the encouragement of many of the club's members, Shippen, along with Bunn, entered the United States Open Championship.

But on the day prior to the start of the competition, controversy threatened to close the Open door and the golfing fate of the two young Americans hung in the balance. Irate that the field included an African-American and a Native American, the foreign-born contingent cornered Theodore Havemeyer, president of the USGA. They told Havemeyer, in no uncertain terms, that if

*The **Shinnecock Hills Golf Club** clubhouse, shown here at the turn of the century, was designed by famed architect Stanford White.*

Shippen and Bunn were allowed to play in the championship, they would not. Havemeyer was just as adamant that Shippen and Bunn would be allowed to play, even if their inclusion inspired the rest of the field to withdraw. It is believed that the president assuaged the dissidents by claiming Shippen was half Shinnecock Indian, a less distasteful racial cocktail in a country drunk on Jim Crow at a time when the Supreme Court would uphold a prior ruling of separate but equal. Whether Havemeyer was motivated by a desire to right civil wrongs or a devotion to fair play is of little consequence. The fact remains that he stood his ground in the crimson face of adversity. The next day Shippen and Bunn teed it up with the world's best, including Charles Blair Macdonald, highly touted winner of the U.S. Amateur in 1895 at Newport Country Club in Rhode Island—and a leader in the development of golf in America.

Paired with Macdonald, Shippen displayed precise shotmaking and incredible maturity; and at the end of the day his 78 tied him with four others for the top spot, making him the first American-born player to lead a U.S. Open. An embarrassed Macdonald withdrew from the championship after shooting 83. The next day, however, young John's game unraveled on the back nine—specifically the par-four 13th where he drove onto a sandy road and hacked his way to an 11. The result was a final-round 81 and a 36-hole total of 159, seven worse than that of Scottish-born winner James Foulis.

Charles Blair Macdonald, winner of the 1895 U.S. Amateur.

Theodore Havemeyer, president of the USGA in 1895.

Shippen never forgot his brush with history, recounting the haunting experience in a *Tuesday* magazine article in 1969. "It was a little, easy par-four. I'd played it many times and I knew I just had to stay on the right side of the fairway with my drive. Well, I played it too far to the right and the ball landed in a sand road. Bad trouble in those days before sand wedges. I kept hitting the ball along the road, unable to lift it out of the sand and wound up with an unbelievable eleven for the hole. You know, I've wished a hundred times I could have played that little par-four again." He received $10 and affirmation of his playing ability, small consolation in the harsh light of retrospection. He played in four more U.S. Opens but was never again a serious contender for the title.

Years later scholars discerned that John Shippen may very well have been the first American-born golf professional, by the USGA's strict interpretation of amateur status. His ethnicity, however, was a little more complicated. Havemeyer's explanation to the mutinous professionals endured, and for a long time historians concluded that Shippen was part Shinnecock Indian. It was not until Marino Parascenzo, a writer for the *Pittsburgh Post-Gazette*, interviewed Shippen's daughter, Clara Shippen Johnson, for a story on her father in advance of the Open's return to Shinnecock Hills in 1986, that his true ethnicity was exposed. Mrs. Johnson said unequivocally that her father was a black man and her mother a full-blooded Indian. Parascenzo alerted a USGA media official and the record was finally set straight.

Although opportunities to compete against white professionals were virtually non-existent outside USGA events, Shippen remained a respected player and teacher, competing on the fledgling United Golfers Association circuit in the '20s and '30s. He worked at a succession of club pro jobs in Washington, D.C., Maryland, New Jersey and New York before securing the position

James Foulis, winner of the 1896 U.S. Open.

Second United States Open Championship
Shinnecock Hills Golf Club, Shinnecock, New York
July 18, 1896

Finish	Entrant	Score		
		First Round	Second Round	Total
1	James Foulis, Chicago	78	74	152
2	Horace Rawlins, Sadaquada	79	76	155
3	G. Douglas, Brookline	79	79	158
	A.W. Smith *, Toronto	78	80	158
5	John Shippen, Shinnecock Hills	78	81	159
	H.J. Whigham *, Onwentsia	82	77	159
7	Joe Lloyd, Essex	78	82	160
	W. Tucker, St. Andrews	78	82	160
9	R.B. Wilson, Shinnecock Hills	82	80	162
10	A. Ricketts, Albany	80	83	163

*Amateur

of greenskeeper and head pro in 1932 at black-owned Shady Rest Country Club in Scotch Plains, N.J. His brother, Cyrus, also attained a certain status as teacher/player. Living in an apartment above the clubhouse at Shady Rest, Shippen served the club in those capacities until it was ceded to the Township of Scotch Plains in 1964. Four years later, John Shippen died in a rest home in Newark, N.J.

John Shippen, after his playing career, became the pro/greenskeeper at Shady Rest Country Club in New Jersey.

The golf world's eyes focused on Shinnecock Hills in July of 1995 as the club hosted the centennial U.S. Open and once again another talented brownskinned teenager colored the landscape. Tiger Woods, who would win a second consecutive U.S. Amateur Championship at Newport CC two months later, prowled the links with comparable pride. Paired with Ernie Els and Nick Price in the premier threesome, Woods injured his wrist attempting to play a recovery shot from knee-high love grass and was forced to withdraw in the second round. But for a brief time, golf's present planted his feet in the footprints of golf's past and history tipped its hat as they walked by.

*Amateur **Tiger Woods** at the 1995 U.S. Open at Shinnecock Hills Golf Club.*

THE FIRST TEE

While John Shippen's baptism by fire at Shinnecock Hills served as a caveat to golf's gatekeepers that the game was not their sacred right, other African-Americans took a quieter, less traveled route to the first tee box. Dr. George Franklin Grant, a successful Boston dentist, was one of them.

Grant was born in 1846 in Oswego, N.Y. Unlike Shippen and many modern-day heroes, his contribution to the game was through ingenuity and resourcefulness rather than playing ability. Grant received a patent for the golf tee in 1899. His was the blueprint for today's wooden and plastic tees. He owned the first patent and also the last recognition for his invention.

By all accounts, Dr. Grant was not the most skilled golfer, but he enjoyed the recreational aspects of the game. He was a gentleman and a scholar, having graduated in Harvard University's second class in dentistry in 1870. A leading authority on the cleft palate, Dr. Grant developed a thriving dental practice. And like many dentists today, he spent much of his down time playing golf. Grant found the method of teeing up a ball—pinching damp sand into a launching pad—both inconsistent and tedious. How could a player determine the preferred height of sand each time? Besides, the

No. 638,920.

G. F. GRANT.
GOLF TEE.
Application filed July 1, 1899.

Patented Dec. 12, 1899.

(No Model.)

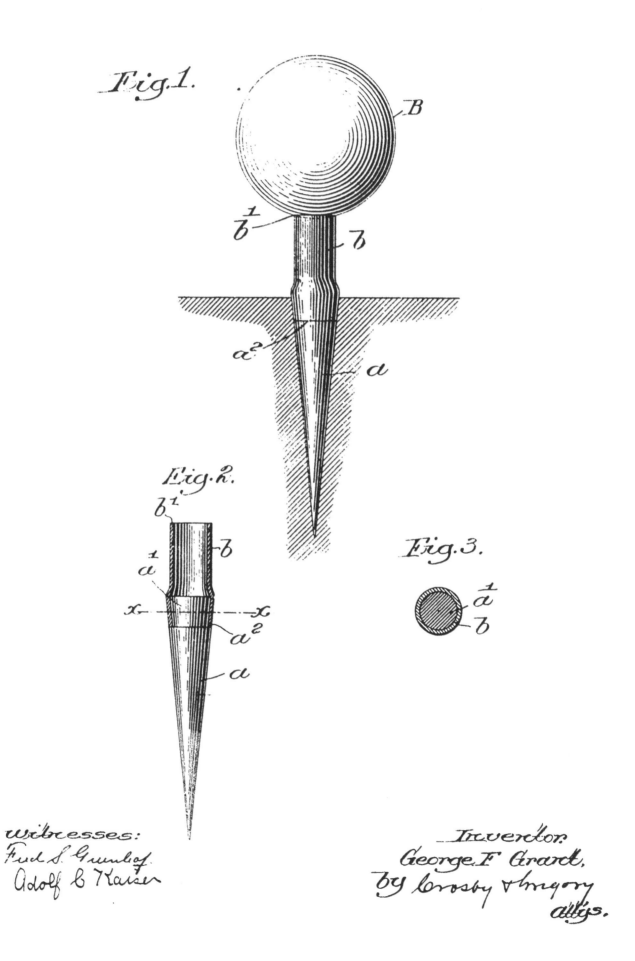

Fig.1.

Fig.2.

Fig.3.

Witnesses:
Fred S. Greenleaf.
Adolf C. Kaiser

Inventor:
George F. Grant,
by Crosby & Gregory
attys.

constant bending over at every tee box to form the little mounds was both physically taxing and, on rainy and inclement days, messy. Appearance, after all, was just as important as a well-struck drive to a gentleman golfer.

So, tired of the inconvenience, Dr. Grant used his skills to improve the game. In 1899, the U.S. Patent Office granted patent 638,920 to George F. Grant of Boston. Grant's tee was described as "a rigid base portion and an attached flexible head, the base being preferably made of wood and tapering to a point at its lower end to be readily inserted in the ground...(the tee had a rubber head with annular seat) on which the ball rests as in a cup...when the ball is struck, the head will yield in the direction of the travel of the ball, offering no obstruction to its flight."

> Dr. Lowell...persuaded the great Walter Hagen... to use his tees during their great barnstorming exhibitions.

But Dr. Grant was more innovator than businessman, more philanthropist than Fuller Brush salesman. He never marketed his invention. He gave some of the tees—manufactured in a small shop in the Boston suburb of Arlington Heights—to friends and playing partners, but the majority of them were squirreled away at his residence. Recalled his daughter, Frances, "He loved challenges, but once he overcame them, he lost interest and moved on to something else." When he died in 1910 at his vacation home in New Hampshire, his invention apparently died with him.

Ten years later, the messy, wet sand tee was still in vogue when Dr. William Lowell, a Maplewood, N.J., dentist, made the late-in-life discovery that golf possessed certain therapeutic advantages. Like Grant, however, the meticulous doctor found no pleasure in soiling his fancy haberdashery during a leisurely round of golf. Dr. Lowell's initial attempt at the golf tee was made of gutta-percha, a material used to make false teeth and golf balls in the 19th century. However, the rubbery material was brittle and broke too easily. Dr. Lowell found white birch to be more durable and manufactured 5,000 tees from it. His first products were colored green, but he soon changed to red dye, and derived the trade name "Reddy Tees" from their color.

An enthusiastic entrepreneur, Dr. Lowell sought to turn red into green. In 1922, he persuaded the great Walter Hagen and one of his fellow professionals, Joe Kirkwood (reportedly with a $1,500 incentive), to use his tees during their barnstorming exhibitions around the country. Hagen described the pandemonium created when they used the tees and left them on the tee box at an exhibition at the Shennecossett Club in Groton, Conn.: "Kids scrambled on the course grabbing them as souvenirs. They became so popular that the club found it necessary to rope off the tees and

The Reddy Tee, the first commercially successful golf tee.

The original patent for the first golf tee.

fairways to control the gallery." It might have been the first time in U.S. golf history that gallery ropes were used.

The Reddy Tee was not patented until May 13, 1925, but three years earlier Dr. Lowell cut a deal with the A.G. Spalding Company, which initially bought 24 dozen. By 1925, profits soared in excess of $100,000. The following year, however, a flood of brands hit the marketplace and Dr.

> Bartholomew was fortunate to come under the tutelage of architect extraordinnaire Seth Raynor, who himself had trained under Charles Blair Macdonald…

Lowell spent much of his remaining years and fortune fighting a losing battle over patent infringement. He died in 1954 at the age of 91. Ironically, it was not until 1991 that the USGA recognized Dr. Grant as the original inventor of the wooden tee. Like a golfer oblivious to time, validity can take an eternity.

BREAKING GROUND

The treelined fairways of New Orleans' Joseph M. Bartholomew Memorial Golf Course beckon the disenfranchised and those born on the southside of the Emerald City's railroad

Pontchartrain Park dedication on May 11, 1956. (Left to right) **James Holtry**, **Joe Bartholomew** *(golf pro),* Mayor **"Chep" Morrison**, *and* **Herbert Jehncke** *(New Orleans Parks Commission).*

tracks. True to their design, the crowned greens repel the fiercest downpour from the heavens while welcoming the heaviest hoof of the downtrodden. There are no asphalt or gravel cart paths, just a green pasture for the game's least likely to be led away from Everyman's salvation—the public course. Like gumbo, and indeed New Orleans itself, Bartholomew GC is a spicy mix of cultures and backgrounds. As the millennium approached, its loyal customers could still tour the 18 holes along Lake Pontchartrain for $7.75 each, less than the price of admission to a putt-putt layout at some theme parks. Affordable, unassuming golf with a color-me-brother attitude. That's how the course's namesake conceived it during a time in America when a non-white could use his genius and muscle to construct a golf course, but dare not attempt to play it for fear of physical harm. Joseph Manuel Bartholomew had bootstrap determination and boardroom savvy. The course stands as a testament to his perseverance in the face of that fear and against all odds.

Born August 1, 1881, in New Orleans, Joe Bartholomew soothed his restless soul with Catholic dogma and an acquisitiveness wrought from youthful exuberance. While in grade school, Bartholomew's enterprising nature thrust him into the workforce and set the tone for what would be a lasting legacy. He began his journey into the annals of golf as a seven-year-old caddie at nearby Audubon Golf Course. Just like Shippen and others before him whose introduction to the game was through the service avenue, young Joe began an instant courtship with golf. He copied the swings of those for whom he caddied, taught himself the game's nuances and quickly became proficient enough to instruct others. He loved the game's freedom of expression, a paradox of enormity in context of the back-door climate involving Coloreds prevalent in the Old South. There were societal parameters that kept one from becoming Bayou bait, and Joe quickly learned those, too. His acceptance as a hard worker who didn't make waves landed him other positions at the exclusive club. He worked on the course's maintenance crew and repaired golf clubs. He became such a good player—he once shot 62 at Audubon—that club members backed him in arranged matches. Joe played against some of the game's greats, including Walter Hagen, Gene Sarazen and Audubon head pro Fred McLeod, winner of the 1908 U.S. Open. Bartholomew also developed a talent for club making. Still, his calling would not be revealed until several years later when he took his talents across town to Metairie Golf Club, whose private membership represented the best and worst of New Orleans' ruling class.

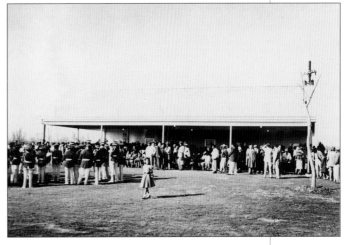

*The opening ceremonies at **Pontchartrain Park**, the New Orleans public course designed by Joe Bartholomew. It was later renamed for him.*

As is sometimes the case, one of the best—in this instance a wealthy Metairie member named H.T. Cottam—extended a hand across racial lines and lifted up a talented individual. Highly impressed with Bartholomew's talents in greenskeeping, Cottam persuaded the club to send Bartholomew to New York to obtain knowledge and experience in golf course architecture. Bartholomew was fortunate to come under the tutelage of architect extraordinnaire Seth Raynor, who himself had trained under Charles Blair Macdonald, before going on to build such outstanding layouts as Blind Brook (in New York), Camargo Club (in Ohio) and Fox Chapel (in Pennsylvania). Early in 1922, Bartholomew returned to New Orleans and began construction of Metairie's new course.

So remote was the location that it could not be reached by any other mode of transportation except horse-drawn wagon. Its isolation, however, did not deter Bartholomew's secrecy. So covetous of his design

Seth Raynor, one of America's greatest golf course architects, tutored Joe Bartholomew in golf course design.

was he that he often worked through the night to protect the project from those who might attempt to steal his ideas. That practice also perturbed some of the Metairie membership, who wanted proof their money was being well spent. One morning, Bartholomew loaded the doubting Thomases into wagons and showed them his progress. They were astounded by the precision of his work. Joe had learned Raynor's style well, as Metairie's generous fairways, well-placed bunkers and crowned greens attested. Not only was his design as beautiful as any in the area, it established an early standard for playability. The members responded by increasing Joe's salary. The payment, however, was limited to monetary value and not human equality. After months of physical labor and mental anguish to see the project to fruition, Bartholomew's creation was off limits to its creator. He wasn't allowed to hit one golf ball on the greenery his mind and hands had shaped.

New Orleans' annual **Mardi Gras** *festival. Bartholomew was active in it and other civic activities.*

Bartholomew found comfort in his family and faith. He married Ruth Segue in 1918 and fathered twins Ruth and Leontine two years later. A son, Joseph M. Bartholomew Jr., was born to the couple in 1925. Joe didn't retreat to his home in the middle-class section of the city known as Carrollton. He remained at Metairie in various capacities and plotted his strategy. After a few years, he moved on to New Orleans Country Club, where he served as head greenskeeper. Over the next decade he built a number of courses in Louisiana, including City Park No. 1, City Park No. 2 and Pontchartrain Park in New Orleans. He also designed and constructed layouts in Covington, Hammond, Abita, Algiers Springs and Baton Rouge, among other cities. However, the public courses, like the City Park playgrounds, were segregated, and Joe, although he built them, could not play them. During that period, Bartholomew received little if any remuneration for several of the courses he built. His biggest payoff came in the form of seven holes he constructed primarily for his African-American friends on property he owned in the New Orleans suburb of Harahan. Unconfirmed but totally believable is the report that Bartholomew never finished the course because the City of Harahan refused to sell him additional land.

As a fortysomething, Bartholomew no longer played competitively, nor did he restrict his energies to building golf courses. He started a construction company and expanded his business into other areas, including landscaping. As the years went by his wealth grew, derived from successful real estate investments and diversified assets. He owned insurance and ice cream companies and gave generously to many New Orleans civic organizations. His contributions to Dillard and Xavier Universities endeared him to the academic community. Neither a social butterfly nor a shrinking violet, Bartholomew joined other prominent African-American men in starting the Original Illinois Carnival Club, an organization founded for the purpose of participation in Mardi Gras festivities. His multifaceted life did not exclude faith. Said his daughter, Ruth, "None of us played golf but we would go with him to the course he owned every Sunday after we got out of church. He loved [his church] and was a very active member. He gave one of the stained glass windows."

> Joe Bartholomew never strayed far from his first love. He was a fixture at Pontchartrain Park well into his 70s.

Joe Bartholomew never strayed far from his first love. He was a fixture at Pontchartrain Park well into his 70s. Even in declining health his eyes would light up at the mention of the game. In 1971, Bartholomew fell victim to a stroke and on Oct. 12 of that year, he died. His legacy, however, lives on.

Bartholomew became the first African-American to be inducted into the Greater New Orleans Sports Hall of Fame in 1972. Seven years later, on a sultry summer day, city officials renamed Pontchartrain Park Golf Course, by now integrated, in his honor. Two of them, Mayor Ernest N. Morial and chief administrative officer Reynard Rochon, were African-Americans. From the links to the political arena, New Orleans' metamorphosis was inspired by men of vision and courage such as Joe Bartholomew. But while the winds of change shout his name around the gazebo outside the clubhouse at Bartholomew Golf Course, it is but a whisper at Metairie. Old prejudices and values die hard.

The first tee at **Pontchartrain Park Golf Course**.

CHAPTER 3

THE SHADOW PEOPLE

"There's an honor in service, and you don't have to look under the dust to find it."
—*Frank Carpenter, longtime club steward at Augusta National Golf Club, April 1998.*

Just like Shippen and Bartholomew, most African-Americans were introduced to the game through positions of service. For them, gaining a toehold of equality proved almost as much of a journey in golf as it was in society as a whole. However, there has long been a common misconception about African-Americans and their connection to golf through service positions. It is true that in many cases the work was demeaning, but certain positions held by blacks—head chef and club steward, in particular—at America's country clubs elevated one's social status in the black community. Often overlooked and underappreciated, service people were an important element in the game's evolution.

Donald Ross and caddie Hard Rock Robinson at Pinehurst.

Some of the most successful African-American players got their start as caddies. Many others were lifelong fixtures around the caddie quarters, earning minimum wage for maximum labor. Some were promoted to caddiemaster, middle management in title only. Others were employed by the club in various domestic capacities. They cooked, cleaned, shined shoes and served the members with loyalty normally reserved for family. In the South, where the industrial revolution had less of an immediate impact, especially for job-seeking minorities, the country club provided opportunities. The work also was clean, honest and often satisfying.

Career caddies, in particular, bled gutta-percha, then surlyn and steel. They were more than bag toters. They were students of the game in tune with nature. A good caddie could be more important to a competitor than his favorite mashie. Clubs like Pinehurst in the sandhills of North Carolina were the stages where they played out their fantasies without benefit of curtain call or deviation from supporting roles and simplistic lifestyles. They arrived at the course before sunup and toiled, typically carrying two golf bags as many as 54 hilly holes, until sundown. Hard labor and hard times strolled life's fairways hand in hand. It was a bearable twosome only in con-

John Henry Williams, the caddiemaster at Augusta.

Young caddies at Pinehurst on their way to work.

text of an often unbearable period in our history—a period where people of color dealt with the effects of racism on a daily basis.

Career caddies, in particular, bled gutta-percha, then surlyn and steel. They were more than bag toters. They were students of the game in tune with nature.

Against a backdrop of exclusion, African-Americans struggled to find acceptance in golf. Some, such as career country club caddie Robert (Hard Rock) Robinson and professional caddie Herman Mitchell, discovered it outside the clubhouse; others, such as club steward Frank Carpenter, earned acceptance from the inside. Both routes took patience and dedication to service.

•

Robinson came into this world a malleable manchild on New Year's Day of 1914 in Camden, S.C., where thoroughbreds freely frolicked and sharecroppers survived on borrowed land. His father moved the family to North Carolina when Robert was 8, settling in Pinehurst, where he found work as a handy man and lawn

Nicklaus and Augusta National caddie on the way to victory in 1975. Until 1983, Masters participants were required to use club caddies.

caretaker. Boston soda fountain magnate James Walker Tufts had purchased 5,500 acres of timberland at approximately $1 an acre in 1895 and begun development of what would become the Pinehurst Resort & Country Club. A haven for the rich and famous, Pinehurst epitomized luxurious living and social splendor with the Carolina Hotel as its centerpiece accommodation. It attracted in its first decade the usual high societal suspects, the Rockefellers, DuPonts and Morgans. Known as the "Queen of the South" and the "White House of Golf," the hotel boasted 250 elegantly furnished rooms and 49 suites with bath. Each room had a telephone and electric lights. Such were Pinehurst's high standards of quality at the turn of the century. Few Southern homes were as well equipped with mod-

*Masters winners **Byron Nelson** (left) and **Gay Brewer** with their caddies at Augusta National.*

The original clubhouse at Pinehurst.

ern technology. But Pinehurst didn't become the prototype for America's playgrounds until Scottish golf course architect Donald Ross arrived in 1901 for what would be a 48-year stay. Ross designed four courses at Pinehurst, including the celebrated Pinehurst No. 2 layout which would host many high-profile championships. During five decades Ross was credited with designing more than 400 courses in North America. As superintendent of Pinehurst Country Club, his duties included establishing caddie fees, which in 1916 were 50 cents for 18 holes for one bag and 70 cents for 18 holes for two bags. Gratuity was a matter of individual generosity.

A person would not get rich caddieing but it was a viable alternative to long hours in the tobacco fields or the tannery. Hard Rock, given that moniker by his father because of the youngster's love of hard rock candy, gravitated to Pinehurst CC as a preadolescent. It provided a welcome alternative to school, of which he wasn't enamored. He started as a shag boy—a practice ball retriever—which wasn't so bad as long as the player was highly skilled and accurate. A novice or intermediate level player provided more challenges, not the least of which was dodging errant shots. Hard Rock loved being around the ladies and gentlemen of leisure as much as the money he took home at the end of the day. His good-natured demeanor met

Though a man couldn't expect to get rich caddying, it was a more appealing job than harvesting tobacco or working in tanneries.

with the approval of Ross, who made Hard Rock his personal caddie the two or three times a week he played. The young man also ran errands for Ross and he did housework. "I was an assistant to Donald Ross," bragged Robinson. "I did anything he told me." Hard Rock became one of the club's most knowledgeable caddies and looped for greats Ben Hogan and Sam Snead, among others, in the North & South Open Championship. It was a sister event to the North & South Men's Amateur, a legendary

Caddies putting on a sand green at Pinehurst.

competition so named because golfers would stop at Pinehurst in the spring on their way north and again in the fall on their way south. In making the transition from youngster to professional

Sam Snead with his caddie at Pinehurst.

career caddie, Hard Rock and Pinehurst's dozens of other staff caddies became as much a part of the club as the "Putter Boy" statue, which stood outside the Pinehurst clubhouse, as one of golf's most recognizable logos.

Celebrities and foreign diplomats frequented the resort. Hard Rock fancied himself an entertainer and would kick up his heels with residents and visitors alike. He claims to have tap danced with Bill (Bojangles) Robinson and given actress Gloria Swanson a few lessons in swivel-hipped swing dancing. Hard Rock's proudest claim to fame, however, remains the relationship he enjoyed with Ross. "Mr. Ross was a Scotsman and a fair man," said Robinson, a regular at Pinehurst until the late '50s when he developed eye problems. "He used to call me 'White Rock.' He could hit the ball, too, just like most of them boys, only sometimes he didn't know where it was going. I thought I was the luckiest man in the world. Sometimes he would ask me, 'White Rock, how do you like it?' I'd say, 'I like it just fine as long as you hit the ball straight.' He'd smile and we'd go on."

A young *Jack Nicklaus* and caddie at the Masters.

Vision problems curtailed Robinson's caddie career and by the early 1950s he was pretty much finished as a Pinehurst regular. During the same period, the residential section off the 17th hole at Pinehurst No. 3 that locals called "Smoke," where most blacks lived, was thriving. So was the club's caddie population, which now numbered more than 500 regulars and part-timers in season. With President Dwight Eisenhower, the country's First Golfer, doing almost as much to popularize the sport as Arnold Palmer would a decade later, country-club membership rolls swelled and prosperity affected the shadow people. Caddies received $2 for a single loop, or about 50 cents an hour, and $3 for two bags.

President Eisenhower used a cart during his rounds at Augusta, but usually employed his caddie, *Frank Partett*, as well.

In the '60s, however, modern technology took a toll on the caddie profession. Club management found golf carts more economically feasible and the caddie population steadily declined. Fewer caddies ultimately translated into fewer African-Americans playing the game recreationally and professionally. A symbolic blow came in 1983, when Augusta National GC stopped requiring Masters participants to use club caddies. The spotlight on the world stage shrunk significantly; as this happened, the glamour associated with caddieing gradually lost its luster. Many caddies persevered by remaining loyal to their home club in season and often migrating to warmer climates during the winter months.

Now 86, Robinson, like millions of other senior citizens, survives on social security and public assistance. Occasionally, a care package from a Pinehurst member will find its way to his residence. The few faithful caddies left at Pinehurst can earn $100 for a single loop. However, 10 times that amount can't replace Robinson's memories of Ross and his sense of belonging to the Pinehurst family. That's priceless.

"Hard Rock" Robinson today, at his home in Pinehurst.

•

Familiarity breeds security. Many country club caddies may have peered through the fence hole but few had the courage or sense of adventure or sheer desperation to explore greener pastures. Herman Mitchell was more the exception than the rule. Born on Oct. 4, 1937, in Little Rock, Ark., Herman and his four siblings personified the pulse of a nation recovering from the Great Depression and preparing for the Great War. They were seeds of hope in a country still searching to achieve equality for all its citizens—what President Franklin D. Roosevelt described as the "forces that drive men apart and forces that draw men together." Herman's father, a Baptist preacher, died when he was 5 and the responsibility of holding a family together fell on the strong shoulders of his mother. Her modest wages from domestic labor provided the necessities for Herman and his siblings, but creature comforts were as scarce in the Mitchell household as cotton in a

Lee Trevino, one half of one of the most enduring player-caddie relationships of modern times.

Little Rock field after harvest. Slim pickings, lean hopes and scant belief that the key to the future could be found in a math primer compelled Herman to drop out of school prior to the seventh grade. Nearby Riverdale Golf Course became his learning center and its members, especially socialites who would lose both their religion and etiquette on a mishit mashie or flubbed pitch shot, became his mentors. A regular double loop at Riverdale netted Herman six dollars, a fortune to a young man determined to supplement his family's income. At 17, Mitchell joined the U.S. Navy, but his military stint lasted not quite two years. His mother died and he received an early discharge to care for his family. Often out of death comes life, and Herman's was about to turn a corner that would eventually lead him to the side of Lee Buck Trevino, a golf icon and, more importantly for Herman, a true friend.

Mitchell soon outgrew Little Rock and headed West to live with relatives in Los Angeles. For months, his search for a job yielded only frustration; then he started hanging around Fox Hill Golf Club, where he met and was befriended by a former PGA Tour caddie nicknamed Texas Sam. By then, in the late '50s, the tour made two or three stops on the West Coast, including the Hesperio Open. Texas Sam took Herman to the tournament and helped him get a loop with a Utah pro named Bill Johnson. Mitchell's career as a professional caddie was launched. Over the next few years, Herman test-drove several players, including Gay Brewer. "I was just trying to jump around and get me a bag to make ends meet," he recalled. He found a regular bag in Gardner Dickinson and caddied for him most of the '60s. Said Mitchell, "He was my daddy, better to me than I was to myself. I loved him almost as much as I love Lee." Dickinson's low tolerance for imperfection in his golf game strained personal and business relationships, but he and Mitchell remained a team for 10 years. When they parted company—amicably—after 10 years, Mitchell found employment with another successful player, Miller Barber, for whom he worked another eight years. Herman again found himself in transition. This time, through an unusual set of circumstances, fate formed a lasting relationship. Trevino, already the winner of two U.S. Opens, was forewarned that his regular caddie, Neil Harvey, would soon quit. He asked Mitchell to caddie for him at the 1976 PGA Championship at Congressional Country Club in Bethesda, Md. They tested the partnership at the Pensacola Open in what turned out to be a rather inauspicious start. "He didn't finish no good," recalled Mitchell. "He kept knocking the ball in the bushes. We didn't beat nobody." During a partnership that would span most of the next two decades, however, Trevino and Mitchell would beat nearly everybody. Their finest hour came in the 1984 PGA Championship at Shoal Creek GC in

> The bond between Mitchell and Trevino was not immediate but it proved enduring … Hulking Herman and swaggering Lee left a lasting impression.

Trevino and *Mitchell* on *the practice tee.*

Jules Alexander

Jules Alexander

Herman Mitchell at the
1990 U.S. Senior Open.

Birmingham, Ala., where Trevino outdueled Gary Player and Lanny Wadkins to capture his sixth and final major championship.

The bond between Mitchell and Trevino was not immediate but it proved enduring. Mitchell, never at a loss for words himself, didn't exactly know what to make of his chatterbox boss. "He shocked me," Mitchell said. "I thought he was crazy when I first met him. Then I found out he's not what he seems on the golf course. Everybody thinks he just talks, talks, talks. Lee's a very private individual. He's very honest, not a phony person." Their partnership, built on trust and dependability, was financially beneficial and mutually satisfying. When Trevino went through several lean seasons in the late 1970s and early 1980s (a result of back problems that traced back to a frightening incident when he was struck by lightning during the Western Open in 1975), Herman never doubted that Trevino would recover. "Lee heals fast," Mitchell said. "He was saying, 'I'm the Bionic Man.'" Had Trevino not recovered sufficiently enough to resume his career, he and Herman would not have become one of the most recognizable player-caddie combos in golf. Hulking Herman and swaggering Lee left a lasting impression.

Mitchell fought a weight problem most of his life. In 1987, he ballooned to 321 pounds. At a tournament in Charlotte, a heckler discovered the extent of Lee's loyalty to his caddie friend. "We were coming to the ninth hole and some white guy yells, 'Hey, Lee, what you feeding that boy?' Lee shot him a look that would kill a bear and said, 'I'm feeding him rednecks and he's getting awful hungry about now.' That guy didn't say another word." Other times, Trevino's levity about Herman's battle with obesity belied his concern over potential health problems. In the early '90s, Trevino took Herman off the bag and sent

Jules Alexander

Trevino and *Mitchell* at
work on the practice tee.
Even during their lean
years, Mitchell stood by
his man.

him to Duke University to undergo a strict weight-loss program. A few years later, Herman retired to Pensacola, Fla., on a pension provided by Trevino. Brotherhood broke down all barriers real or imagined and transformed a poor, young African-American into a man rich beyond worldly possessions. "Caddieing just appealed to me," Mitchell said. "I couldn't wish for no better. I could have made a lot of money if I had had any sense. I made the money. I just blew it. But I still did OK for a man with no education."

Ben Crenshaw and *Carl Jackson* at the Masters in 1995. Crenshaw credited Jackson's pre-tournament swing tip for helping him win.

The Trevino-Mitchell duo was just one of the many successful player-caddie teams that populated the PGA Tour in the 1960s, '70s and '80s; these also included Gary Player and Alfred (Rabbit) Dyer, and Tommy Bolt and (Cutshot) Johnson. In 1995, the world watched in reverential jubilation as Ben Crenshaw fell into the arms of his longtime Masters caddie, Carl Jackson, after Crenshaw won a second green jacket. More representative of the changing times, however, is the small percentage of African-American caddies on the PGA Tour as the game ushered in the 21st century. Only one of the top 50 players in the current world ranking, Hal Sutton, employs an African-American caddie—Freddie Burns. Extinction for blacks, in a service position once considered too demeaning for white Americans, appears inevitable in the professional ranks.

•

Augusta National Golf Club's wine cellar is temperature-controlled to protect the integrity and enhance the aging process of the imported and domestic wines stored there. Until 1975, when Lee Elder became the first African-American to "qualify" for the Masters, people of color were welcome at Augusta National only in uniform—not military, but service. Still, certain positions inside the Augusta National clubhouse, and many other clubhouses around the country for that matter, were accorded high levels of esteem within the black community. Frank Carpenter's job of club steward at Augusta National is one of those positions. The Waynesboro, Ga., native, who oversees Augusta National's world-renowned wine cellar, is as much a master of his profession as the

Crenshaw, overcome with emotion, after winning the 1995 Masters is comforted by *Jackson*. It was their second Masters title together.

players celebrated every April for their shotmaking brilliance among the dogwoods and azaleas. Carpenter is an expert in vintage wines, corporate CEOs and ordinary folk.

"Golfers are very different today," Carpenter says, leaning back in a chair in his office adjacent to the clubhouse kitchen. "They're still competitors but they don't seem to be friendly like the golfers were when I first came here in '53. Hogan won the Masters that year and tied Sam Snead the next year but lost to him in a playoff. They were different personalities. Sam Snead was the extroverted type who liked to tell jokes and have fun. He mingled

Frank Carpenter in the wine cellar at Augusta National. Carpenter has worked at the club since the days of the Roosevelt administration.

with the service people. He had a caddie named O'Brien Williams and at the end of the Masters each year, he'd give O'Brien that trademark straw hat of his. Ben Hogan, on the other hand, was a very serious individual who kept to himself. You wouldn't catch him cracking jokes with the caddiemaster."

Claude Harmon, Jimmy Demaret and Jackie Burke were big tippers. Others, according to Carpenter, "just weren't good to anybody." Cliff Roberts was a connoisseur of fermented grapes, his palate particularly pleased by Chateau Talbot. President Dwight Eisenhower, an Augusta National member, favored 21-year-old Scotch for its smooth texture and taste. Carpenter kept all of them supplied with distilled delights and anything else within his sphere of influence. His long tenure at the club started during the F.D.R. years in the White House, when a few pieces of silver in a young man's pocket mightily lifted his status and self-esteem.

Frank's father was an auto mechanic, his mother a housekeeper. They moved the family to Augusta in 1936 when Frank was 9. Enterprising even as a youngster, Frank worked in his grandfather's tiny store back in Waynesboro during the summers, selling vegetables and other stock. However, he loved the hustle and bustle of downtown Augusta as much as the solitude of the fishing hole back home. Frank was especially intrigued by the young shoeshine boys working the street corners. Before long he talked his mother into allowing him to shine shoes in the neighborhood and at her cousin's barbershop on Saturdays. Earning a nickel for each pair he shined, Frank would labor long and hard each day to reach his goal of five dollars from shop customers. By his teens, he had opened a shoeshine stand in a bar that had a pool hall and gaming room. Frank shined shoes for the gamblers and sometimes came across a few discarded chips during his clean-up. A couple

*Young bellboys at the old **Bon Aire Vanderbilt Hotel** in Augusta, where most of the Masters competitors stayed in the early days of the tournament.*

Charlie Coody won at Augusta in 1971.

A member of the service staff at Augusta National Golf Club watches the action at the Masters.

of years later, he moved on to a cocktail lounge owned by a Chicagoan named Bob Ship. Frank stocked boxes of liquor, shined brass and generally performed the duties of a bar-back until he graduated to bartender. His boss also owned a private club that catered to military officers stationed at Ft. Gordon. "I used to mix drinks for the waiters to serve to the tables," recalled Carpenter. "It was like Las Vegas with slot machines and all kinds of stuff. I used to work that little room, and they would tip big. That's when I started making the big money. I was 18 and could make as much as $200 a week. That was in 1943. I didn't have a car because you could ride anywhere in a cab for 25 cents."

Frank dropped out of school when he got drafted into the Army in 1945. He completed high school in the service, received some vocational training upon being discharged in '47 and got a job at the post office, where he worked for eight years. During that period, Carpenter took on bartending duties part-time at Augusta National. The club's first steward, Bowman Milligan, had complete run of the clubhouse and was Frank's mentor. Carpenter would work the graveyard shift (from midnight until 7 a.m.) at the post office, grab a couple hours sleep and head to the golf club. Milligan set up a refreshment cart between nines and Frank would work it until 5 p.m. Milligan kept after him to quit the post office and work for him full-time. Eventually he relented, and in 1958, Carpenter became head bartender at Augusta National. Each summer, when Augusta National was closed, he found employment at other private clubs, first in Myrtle Beach, S.C., then at Lake Placid, N.Y. There he came under the tutelage of Walter Oliver, service manager of the White Face Inn, a resort hotel in the Adirondacks where high-rollers summered. "[Milligan and Oliver] had two different styles of management," said Carpenter of his teachers. "Oliver was a consummate gentleman. He had a lot of finesse and was very diplomatic. Bowman believed in getting things done at all cost. All he wanted was the end result. I used to tell him when he left I was going to get his job."

That time came sooner than Frank anticipated. In 1972, illness forced Bowman Milligan into retirement and Frank stepped into a position he had coveted for years. He hand-picked his staff from chef to maitre d'. Turning the wine cellar, constructed in 1954 under orders from Roberts, into a world-class facility became his top priority. "When I came here, I didn't know anything about wine," Carpenter said. "I got it from reading and exposure." He made several trips to vineyards and wineries in Northern California and a couple to France. He became an expert in vintage ports and now advises Masters champions on a choice of wine to accompany their selected menu for the traditional pre-tournament dinner attended by past champs only. For example when Tiger Woods hosted the feast in 1998, Car-

> Carpenter's stoic facade masked the pride that he and Augusta National's other service stars shared in Woods' breakthrough victory. Like a raised glass of champagne to a champion of color in the privacy of a stolen moment, they basked in his glory, too.

penter selected a white Burgundy, Batard-Montrachet Grand Cru, 1995 vintage, and a red Chateau Mouton Rothschild, 1975 vintage, to wash down Woods' choice of cheeseburger and fries. There was also symbolic value to the wine. The vintages were in honor of Tiger's first visit to Augusta National (in 1995) and the year of his birth ('75). "As host, we wanted to do something special for him," said Carpenter through a sheepish smile.

Carpenter's stoic facade masked the pride that he and Augusta National's other service stars shared in Woods' break-through victory. Like a raised glass of champagne to a champion of color in the privacy of a stolen moment, they basked in his glory, too. A nod between the knowing confirmed what they believed long before Elder first walked on the hallowed grounds of the National. Given an opportunity, black golfers would compete with the best of them.

In the quiet of his study at home, Carpenter often reflects on a lifetime of serving others. His wife has long since stopped fussing about his fanaticism over organization and regimentation. Like the fine wine he collects for Augusta National, he has aged well. "Bowman told me when I was coming up that you always gain the respect of important people, these kinds of people," he said, pointing to the Masters gathering outside the clubhouse. "You don't have to worry about what other people think of you. When you get the respect of the highest type of people, that's when it means something to you. And I find that to be true."

*President Eisenhower, the president's military aide, **Bowman Milligan** and **Cliff Roberts** at Augusta National.*

CHAPTER 4

A PLACE OF THEIR OWN

"We just said our prayers that he would do well. He was a standard bearer. We finally got one in."
—Former United Golfers Association president Porter Pernell, on Lee Elder making it to the Masters in 1975.

Long before a PGA Tour card became a gold carrot and platinum passport to prosperity, those who aspired to play golf professionally were considered foolhardy souls with an aversion to dirty fingernails and sweaty brows. White club pros, those loosely organized by wealthy merchant Rodman Wanamaker in 1916 under the Professional Golfers Association of America banner, were viewed—initially, anyway—as mere vagabonds playing for miniscule purses on a winter circuit that served as a sidelight to their real jobs. Amateurs held a higher place in golf's pecking order—they were called "gentlemen" and treated like the game's true champions. African-American golf enthusiasts, both recreational and seriously competitive, were persona non grata. There is no evidence that the early overtures of John Shippen and others made anything but scant significance toward opening up the game to people of color. In fact, it was not until African-Americans decided to form the United Golfers Association (UGA) and, later, the North American Golfers Association, that they began to alter the game's landscape in this country.

Both organizations, microcosms of the black community, would develop worthy champions and citizens. Some of them, most notably Charlie Sifford, Lee Elder, Jim Dent and Jim Thorpe, rose from those obscure circuits to places of prominence on the PGA Tour. Others, such as John Brooks Dendy and Robert (Pat) Ball, gave the UGA legitimate star power during its formative years and helped stabilize the UGA's foundation for those who came after them. Even though they have endured mostly by sketchy recall, their stories, and that of the organizations impacted by them, are no less intriguing.

Early on, John Brooks Dendy was influenced by a creative process African-American elders have referred to with only a modicum of self-deprecation as "Ethiopian ingenuity." In a literal sense, it refers to the art of making something out of nothing or making the best use of what you have. As a 12-year-old in the roaring '20s, smitten with a game considered a pursuit for the privileged, Dendy had to use every bit of his imagination to fashion a set of golf clubs. He collected several metal clubheads but had no shafts with which to connect head and grip—a situation akin to having a car with no motor. So he took some discarded broomhandles and a case knife and whittled them down to a more flexible thickness. He fitted one

John Brooks Dendy, one of the first great stars of the United Golfers Association. He won the Negro National Open in 1932, 1936 and 1937.

end in the club head and shaved the other in the manner of a grip. Dendy, whose parents moved the family from Laurens, S.C., to Asheville, N.C., played with those homemade relics for several years. He would eventually become a three-time Negro National Open champion but not before others stout in spirit and determination organized to give people of color a proving ground.

At the time Dendy was learning to play golf with his improvised set of clubs, major league baseball was closed to African-Americans. Opportunities for blacks in the slowly forming National Football League weren't much better. And American golf was no more eager to fraternize with people of color than baseball and football. The United States Golf Association had no written policy either espousing or damning segregation but, despite the John Shippen display at the 1896 U.S. Open, by the 1920s blacks and other non-whites were not welcomed at USGA events. As a result, most shied away from the USGA's forbidden fields.

Although the PGA's "Caucasian-only clause" barring non-whites from participating in PGA-sanctioned events wasn't written into the organization's bylaws until 1934, blacks were, in effect, shunned and discouraged from participating in PGA tournaments. However, a light-skinned African-American named Dewey Brown found a way to circumvent the PGA's rigid racial non-policy. Brown was born in rural North Carolina near the turn of the century and started caddieing at an early age after his family moved to New Jersey. He quickly developed as a player but showed even more promise as a clubmaker. He fashioned clubs for socialites as well as some of the game's top players, including Chick Evans, who used a set made by Brown to win the 1916 U.S. Amateur. Brown also became a respected golf instructor, working with renowned professional Willie Norton at Shawnee-on-the-Delaware in eastern Pennsylvania. In 1928, he secured membership in the PGA of America. He was a dues-paying member of the organization until 1934, when his membership was suddenly and inexplicably terminated. That same year the PGA of America added the following amendment to its constitution, Article III, Section I: "Professional golfers of the Caucasian Race and their assistants, over the age of eighteen years and residing in North America or South America, who have served at least three years in the profession (either in the employ of a golf club or as an assistant to a qualified professional), shall be eligible for election to membership, and in addition thereto the Association, in representative assembly, may elect any number of honorary members and from said honorary members may elect an honorary president and not to exceed two honorary vice-presidents." The timing of the amendment could have been a coincidence, but it is a certainty that Brown fit the PGA's criteria for membership in every respect but one. Apparently, his lack of pigmentation no longer masked his true ethnicity. He was outed, literally. Brown served at numerous clubs in New Jersey before his death in 1973, 12 years after the Caucasian-only clause was eliminated from the PGA's constitution.

Shippen's encounter with resistance on the links might have been the first recorded incident but it was far from the last. Fourteen years after the near rebellion at Shinnecock Hills, a Chicagoan named Walter Speedy and three playing partners were denied entrance to a city-run tournament. The four sued Chicago park officials for not allowing them to play. The lawsuit failed to blast away any prejudices or social injustices; ultimately, African-Americans knew they could find acceptance among themselves, and that was the impetus for a meeting in the 12th Street branch of the Washington (D.C.) YMCA on a late summer day in 1925—a coming together of men of similar mind that would galvanize the game into parallel if not equal access and opportunity.

Washington, D.C.'s, Lincoln Memorial in 1924. The nearby Lincoln Memorial Golf Course hosted one of the first national tournaments for black golfers.

Attending the meeting that day was an eclectic group of African-Americans, answering the call to unite in the struggle to construct a home for minority golfers. The official press release defined their purpose simply: "The object of the national organization is to gather all colored golfers and golf associations into one body." Some historians credit Robert H. Hawkins, owner of Mapledale GC in Stow, Mass., with the vision for a united front. Others suggest his role was more supportive than one of leadership. Regardless of who actually spearheaded the effort, it is beyond debate that the Colored Golfers Association of America or the United States Colored Golfers Association—the original name has been disputed over the years— was born from that meeting. Shady Rest G&CC president B.C. Gordon was elected to preside over the new organization and a spate of recognized competitions under the auspices of a single ruling body was discussed. African-Americans had conducted tournaments prior to the USCGA. One of the first events was sponsored by the Alpha Golf Club and held in 1915 at Marquette Park Golf Course in Chicago. Speedy, one of the top black golfers of that era, won the tournament. Nine years later, on a resplendent autumn day at Lincoln Memorial Golf Course in Washington, D.C., some of the finest black golfers on the East Coast matched skills for an assortment of trophies. Riverside Golf Club and its president, Victor R. Daly, sponsored the tournament that, as one newspaper account reported, garnered "a great deal of interest both locally and nationally." Captain and Mrs. R.C. Clayton defeated Daly and his partner, A. Mae Stewart, 1 up, in the mixed foursomes. Schoolteacher Brenda Moryck won the women's division and J.H. Scott Jr. captured the men's title.

> From its inception the UGA was structured to represent the growing African-American golfing community … this black-run golf body was every bit as serious about the game as the USGA and the PGA of America.

Shady Rest was the site of the first National Colored Golf Championship over the Fourth of July weekend in 1925. Located in the New York City bedroom community of Westfield, N.J., the club attracted large galleries and the top talent from New York, Connecticut, Pennsylvania, Long Island and the District of Columbia. The final round pairing of John Shippen and Harry Jackson of Washington, D.C., produced a dramatic finish. Jackson, much younger than his more heralded opponent, shot a 72-hole total of 299 to edge Shippen by three strokes and top the 30-player field. Jackson won $25 and instant fame from the detailed reports in black-owned newspapers such as the New York Amsterdam News, Baltimore Afro-American and Chicago Defender. Those messengers were African-Americans' lifeline to their ever-expanding world. The results of predominantly black sporting events rarely warranted even the agate type of major newspapers.

Most of the early black-run tournaments were generally the showcase of the host club and fostered more of a social than a competitive environment. USCGA-sanctioned events, however, were an innovative umbrella approach to bringing separate parts together for the benefit of the whole. The founding fathers decided to hold a national championship the following year at Mapledale over Labor Day weekend. The event was given "open" status, which meant amateurs and professionals were eligible to compete in the two-day, 72-hole tournament for a $4 entry fee. Heavy rains threatened to wash out the event but the 38 competitors from 10 states withstood the inclement weather and soggy conditions. Jackson again prevailed in the pro division with a 295, four shots better than Chicagoans Robert (Pat) Ball and Porter Washington. Shippen finished fourth at 304 and New Jersey's Elmer Stout took fifth at 310. Jackson pocketed $100 while playoff winner Washington collected $75. Third, fourth and fifth places paid $50, $25 and $15, respec-

Robert (Pat) Ball and caddie.

tively. Amateurs in two flights were awarded cups and medals. African-Americans won more than a few dollars and some hardware during that historic 48 hours. They earned an identity in a game still searching for firm footing in this country. It was a priceless commodity considering no amount of green, gold or silver could have purchased a place for an African-American alongside Walter Hagen or Gene Sarazen or any of the PGA's pioneers.

*As a boy, Ball caddied for the great **Bobby Jones** (above).*

In 1927, the second of three consecutive years that Mapledale hosted the national championship, Ball, a former caddie who migrated to the Midwest from Atlanta, torched the field with a 293 score and a 20-shot victory. Shippen finished second and Jackson third. The $300 purse paid 12 places, including $100 to Ball, who earlier that year had defeated Tommy Thompson in the Cook County Open. That triumph by Ball, over one of Chicago's top white players in the 36-hole final, was a combination of power and finesse. One newspaper account said, "Ball's driving was the most remarkable seen lately on the Garfield course. From several tees his ball landed directly on the green and in lots of cases went clear over." As an integral figure in the USCGA's formative years, Ball understood how to challenge the system without fanfare, like a mouse in the last church pew. With roots in golf planted deep in the red clay of Georgia, he had country charisma coated with big-city guile. As a young man, Ball caddied for the great American amateur, Bobby Jones, at East Lake GC in Atlanta. It was in that environment of southern gentility, and sometimes hostility, that he quickly learned how to fade into the scenery. Jones demanded that his caddies be fit enough to withstand the Georgia sun, fleet enough to keep pace and respectful enough not to speak unless spoken to. Ball applied those lessons to his life and golf and they served him well.

Program from the North-South Tournament, one of the most prestigious black-run tournaments.

In 1930, a year after the United States Colored Golfers Association changed its name to the United Golfers Association, Ball became the first African-American to enter the prestigious Western Amateur. Curiously, of the 153 players in the qualifying rounds, he was the only one not assigned a playing partner; instead, an official of the Western Golf Association played as his marker. Unperturbed by the subtle slight, he shot an 81 to advance. The next round, however, produced an 83 and an early exit from the tournament. (The Detroit News referred to Ball as "the only Negro to qualify for a major golf championship," further proof that Shippen's true ethnicity had been covered up.) Ball, who won the UGA national championship again in 1929 on the strength of a Shady Rest course-record 66 in the opening round, was also a small businessman. He operated a miniature golf links on Wabash Ave. in

Chicago. His stature both inside and outside the black golf arena grew as the UGA's arteries spread from Chicago to Connecticut.

From its inception the UGA was structured to represent the growing African-American golfing community. The organization was divided into districts to include various black golf clubs around the country. The New England District consisted of clubs in Massachusetts, Connecticut and Rhode Island and the Eastern District took in Washington D.C., New York, New Jersey, Maryland and Pennsylvania. The Midwest District eventually became the largest, encompassing Illinois, Indiana, Michigan, Wisconsin and Kentucky. By 1995, the Midwest District had 21 members, including the Chicago Executive Women, Fairway Golf Club of Dayton, Ohio, and Rivercity Golf Club of Evansville, Ind., to name a few. In the early years, most of the UGA competitions were held at 9-hole and 18-hole municipal courses such as Casa Loma CC in Powers Lake, Wis., Sunset Hills near Kankakee, Ill., Douglass Park in Indianapolis, Rackham in Detroit, Mohansic in New York, Highland Park in Cleveland, Cobbs Creek in Philadelphia, Palos Park in Chicago and Langston in Washington, D.C., site of the Capital City Open. Most of the member organizations were urban-based and events such as the Sixth City Classic of Cleveland and Schaefer Beer Classic of Asbury Park, N.J., had a big-city flavor. As the organization grew, so did its sphere of influence. Brought into the fold were districts representing the central states, plus the Southwest and Southeast sections of the country. The latter was sparsely represented, largely due to segregation and black flight to the North and Midwest by caddies like Ball, who learned the game in the South but ultimately found opportunities to play it almost everywhere else except home. Each district elected officers and conducted competitions. Every two years UGA members chose national officers and voted on issues relevant to the organization. This black-run golf body was every bit as serious about growing the game as the USGA and the PGA of America.

Of course, not all African-American golf enthusiasts fled the South in search of a better chance in the job market or clubhouse. Many stood toe to toe with Jim Crow and refused to blink first. John Brooks Dendy was one of them. With those broomhandle golf clubs, Dendy developed a swing less refined than the passes of the members at Asheville Country Club for whom he caddied, but one that was every bit as effective. By his early teens, he had built a reputation among the other caddies as a gritty competitor. Some of the members began to take note, too. The summer between his graduation from Stephens Lee High School and his freshman year at Paine College in Augusta, Ga., where he would enroll on a football scholarship, Dendy received financial backing from several members to travel to Atlanta to play in the Southern Open at Lincoln G&CC. Though he was just 18 years old, Dendy conquered high winds and difficult sand greens to defeat the best the South had to offer, including homegrown heroes Howard Wheeler, John (Honey) Smith and Hugh Smith. When offered the choice between a handsome trophy and the $50 first-place prize, Dendy opted for the money and turned professional on the spot. He would win the Southern Open again in 1934 and 1936. Although the tournament apparently was not affiliated with the UGA, his success there served as a springboard to the national stage.

> Of course, not all African-American golf enthusiasts fled the South in search of a better chance in the job market or clubhouse. Many stood toe to toe with Jim Crow and refused to blink first.

Later in the summer of '32, friends and family convinced Dendy that he could compete against the UGA's best. Somewhat reluctantly, he boarded a Greyhound bus for the long journey to Indianapolis and the Negro National Open. The event itself was being staged at Douglass Park GC, a nine-hole layout owned by the city and the only refuge for black golfers in Indiana. The course began as a six-hole experiment in 1926, with tomato cans used for cups. Its development grew with interest in the game among African-Americans. Dendy had never ventured that far from home before and the anxiety over being out of his element was understandable. But when he arrived at the golf course, Dendy was in comfortable surroundings. Not even an initial introduction to some of the tour's biggest names caused his focus to wane. To say that his subsequent victory was a shock would be putting it mildly. As a virtual unknown, Dendy had drawn such scant attention that he was one of the last players selected in the pre-tournament "calcutta." He went for $400, but the man who purchased him won several times that amount when Dendy won. The bettor gave the newly crowned champ $500 from his winnings—five times the amount Dendy received for first place. Upon boarding the Greyhound bus for home, Dendy found a window seat and settled in for the long return trip. He never closed his eyes for fear that someone might steal his winnings.

One of the greatest stories regarding Dendy's talent involved a 1933 exhibition in Jacksonville, Fla., in which he was invited to participate. After arriving late because of problems with his bus, Dendy went straight to the first tee. Without warming up, Dendy laced a drive over the dogleg and down the hill toward the green, 342 yards away. When he got to the green, the ball was in the cup. He played the next three holes 2-3-4 (all of them birdies), and finished the round with a score of 59. The 1-2-3-4, six-under-par start, made *Ripley's Believe It Or Not*. Dendy would win the National Open again in 1936 and 1937. He would also meet a fledgling golfer with huge soft hands and a physique chiseled from granite named Joe Louis. The two became friends and golf partners in several successful matches, including a week-long fleecing of some Chicago-area locals the week after Dendy had made an unsuccessful defense of his national title in the summer of 1933. The event was held at

Sunset Hills GC in Kankakee, Ill., but Dendy found lodging in a cost-efficient Chicago hotel. The city overflowed with visitors to that year's World's Fair. The small-town lad was lost among the thousands of faces and more than a little intimidated by the speeding motorists and street hustlers. Perhaps that explains why he kept his hand on his wallet and his mind on his golf the entire time he was in the big city.

By 1940, Dendy had found little financial reward in competitive golf, so he decided to take a full-time job as a locker-room attendant at Asheville Country Club. Shortly afterward, he moved on to nearby Biltmore Forest CC, where he supervised the grill-room and locker room until his retirement in 1980. During that period, Dendy's interest in golf was limited to the occasional casual round with his sons and an annual pilgrimage to the Masters at Augusta National GC as a spectator. He died in March of 1985 from dementia and kidney failure.

By the 1940s, the UGA had become not only the training ground for top African-American golfing talent such as Zeke Hartsfield, Bill Spiller, Teddy Rhodes, Charlie Sifford and Lee Elder, it was a sanctuary for a unique subculture. The black golf tour touched almost every aspect of African-American life. From beauty salons to restaurants, the local business community benefited from the influx of revenue during tournaments. Major corporations supported local events through sponsorships. Some, like the Stroh's Brewery in Detroit, even gave modest financial backing to entire teams. The tour attracted head-line entertainers and professional athletes. Joe Louis, a frequent attendee at UGA events, would stand alongside the circuit's stalwarts as they fought for access to the more lucrative PGA Tour.

Other sports figures, such as boxing's Sugar Ray Robinson, baseball's Jackie Robinson and football's Jim Brown, made regular celebrity appearances at UGA events. Cab Calloway, Count Basie, Duke Ellington and other top bands of the era were booked for the balls and galas that were the very essence of the UGA's social gathering at each tournament. It was not unusual for players and entertainers to mingle. Popular singer Billy Eckstine hired Sifford as a personal instructor and hustling partner in the '50s. Sifford and his comrades on the UGA often made more money in a four-hour hustle than for winning a tournament over three days and 72 holes.

Black golf tournaments were great gathering places for African-American culture in the 1940s and 1950s. (Left to right) **Cab Calloway, Louis Armstrong** *and* **Duke Ellington** *all provided entertainment at UGA events.*

Temple University urban Archives

(Left to right) **Joe Louis,**
Sugar Ray Robinson,
Teddy Rhodes and **Joe**
Roach.

Recalled Sifford in his book *Just Let Me Play*, "When I was traveling with Billy Eckstine in the early '50s, it was hustle or be hustled, because there were cats out there who stood in line to get a piece of Mr. B on the golf course." Sifford portrays Zeke Hartsfield as the greatest set-up man of them all. In his book, Sifford describes how Hartsfield would bait challengers and lighten their wallets. One of the Atlantan's favorite ploys was to hang around the practice green and bet he could two-putt from any distance. He would also sucker in opponents by hitting some rather pedestrian shots, then miraculously recovering to win the bet. Hartsfield was such a great putter that he would pull the blade out from distances normally requiring a short iron and roll the ball with superb distance control. He appeared so lucky that none believed it was actually skill. "Those guys probably would have killed me if they knew I was a professional," Hartsfield said.

George Wallace Jr., a.k.a. Tater Pie, was perhaps the UGA's most infamous con artist. This Atlanta native played cross-handed and his unorthodox style suckered a number of marks. "Tater Pie was a professional gambler," said Rafe Botts, who had a brief stint on the UGA before following Sifford onto the PGA Tour in the early '60s. "He was a country boy and he talked funny. He always had a pocketful of money. He wouldn't expose his game until it was too late for his opponent. He was like a ghost. It was like, who is this guy?"

Before Lee Elder earned a right to play on the PGA Tour, he not only played the UGA circuit but traveled as a caddie for an infamous hustler named Alvin C. Thomas, nicknamed "Titanic Thompson" because of his love for high-stakes

Both football great
Jim Brown and **Jackie**
Robinson, shown here
with his wife Rachel at
the Baseball Hall of
Fame induction ceremo-
ny, made celebrity
appearances at UGA
events.

games. "A lot of times when I couldn't go into the clubhouse, I would make the matches for him," said Elder in an interview with the Boston Globe in 1994. Elder would set the hook among fellow caddies. Other times Thompson would wager that he and his caddie could beat the club's two best players. Lee's pockets were rarely empty in those days. Said Elder, "Ti was a great friend. He was the first white golfer who ever treated me with respect and dignity. I will never forget him."

Whenever Elder and Thompson ventured below the Mason-Dixon line they met with resistance. The UGA, quite frankly, could not establish a foothold in the South because of the segregationist policies which still existed there. For a long time, African-Americans had to be content with caddie play days at country clubs. In the '50s, municipal courses grudgingly opened their fairways to blacks on specified days. That crack in the door led to a groundswell of interest in the game and African-American social clubs finally began to organize and conduct competitions. By the '60s, most Southern states could boast of at least one African-American club and, in 1964, Jekyll Island, Ga., became host to the region's most prominent tournament. That year, businessman Earl Hill organized the Southeastern Open; it was held during Thanksgiving every year thereafter. Much like the UGA's founding fathers, Hill's vision was to bring all of the satellite organizations and their tournaments under one roof. During his tournament in 1968, he met with several officials of other clubs, including Billy Gardenheight, Sam Quick and Charles Collette of the Skyview Golf Association in Asheville, N.C., Thomas (Smitty) Smith, Rev. John (Honey) Smith and Henry Cochran of Atlanta, Oscar Vincent of Macon, Ga., and John Cornelius of Knoxville, Tenn. From that meeting arose the North American Golfers Association, related to the UGA only in that the two organizations shared some of the same players. While the NAGA was regional, the UGA remained the only national entity, with member clubs in every section of the country except the West Coast. An organization known as the Western States Golf Association, chartered in 1954, controlled black golf west of the Rocky Mountains.

Programs from the 1967 North-South and Mid-Winter Opens, key stops on the NAGA circuit. In its heyday, the tour offered first-prize checks of $2,500.

The Southeastern was the prototype for most of the tournaments on the NAGA circuit, which began in early May with the Macon Four-Ball and concluded in November with Hill's event. Just like the UGA, member clubs up the Eastern Seaboard from Eufala, Ala., to Greensboro, N.C., hosted the mostly 54-hole, stroke-play events. The competitions were divided into a Pro Division, Senior Pro Division, Men's Amateur (with up to 10 flights), Senior Amateur and Women's Division. All players paid an entry fee and the pros were paid in cash. Typically, pros put up $100, often pushing the entry deadline to the day of the opening round, for a chance to win a first prize of between $1,200-$2,500, depending upon the number of entries. The tournament paid perhaps 15 places, with only the top finishers able to cover expenses. "Most of us were playing for the competition and because we loved the game," said Joe Roach, who played out of Miami Springs GC, site of the North-South, one of the most prominent black-run events. Once a PGA Tour stop, Miami Springs hosted one of the events that made up Byron Nelson's unprecedented 11-victory streak of 1945. "We had a lot of side bets," added Roach. "That's where the real money was." Purses grew with corporate sponsorship money. By the 1990s, a few of the events on the circuit were paying out $30,000 in prize money—a far cry from the $300 purse of the inaugural UGA National Open but only a token compared to the PGA Tour's multi-million dollar bonanzas. "You can't compare black golfers to the Ben Crenshaws and the Greg Normans because every tournament they go to they've got 'In God We Trust' in their pockets," said veteran black tour member Jesse Allen. "Most tournaments blacks go to they've got 'If The Lord's Willing.'" Allen figures in his best year traversing

> When outside pressure to liberate the game began to take a toll on the PGA Tour in the late '50s, the UGA was there as a clearinghouse and bully pulpit.

the mini-tours, including the UGA and NAGA, he might have won in excess of $30,000. In 1999, Tiger Woods led the PGA Tour in earnings with more than $6 million.

Although the NAGA gave African-Americans more opportunities, the UGA remained the only national organization for people of color. When outside pressure to liberate the game began to take a toll on the PGA Tour in the late '50s, the UGA was there as a clearinghouse and bully pulpit. Said Porter Pernell, activist and former UGA president, "We acted as a conduit for the PGA on a number of occasions when they wanted a character reference on players like Pete Brown, Lee Elder, Rafe Botts and Charlie Sifford. I was personally contacted by Gulf Oil's Roy Kohler when they were looking for a representative to send to South Africa for a tournament. They wanted an African-American. I put them in touch with Lee Elder."

Pernell also flooded PGA headquarters with letters, imploring tour officials to exercise their influence on decision-makers at the Masters, considered African-American golfers' last frontier. "We feel we were instrumental in getting the Masters to change some of their thinking about letting a black in," Pernell said. "The tour's attitude was that the Masters was not a tour event so it was outside their control. We didn't buy that because they were always in attendance at the Masters. We cited the fact that foreigners who were being invited hadn't won any big tournaments. We felt there was a double standard being applied to blacks and that some Afro players should have been invited."

Elder finally received the long-awaited Masters invitation by the green jackets in 1975 after winning the Monsanto Open in Pensacola, Fla., the previous year. "We were jubilant, just elated," Pernell said. Elder, who in 1966 won 18 of the 22 UGA and NAGA events he entered, and all of the other UGA refugees who came before and after him owe a debt of gratitude to the organization's founding fathers and the myriad human pillars who kept the UGA standing. Now 74 years old, the UGA still provides a haven for young hopefuls and graying diehards relentless in their pursuit of the dream. That it and the NAGA have been viable playgrounds for people of color is without question. So is their place in the evolution of golf among African-Americans.

Porter Pernell.

CHAPTER 5

THE PLAYING FIELDS

"We tend to think of integration in positive terms, (but) new generations will not have the kind of rapport, relationship, endearment to a black institution as would those who came up in a segregated, exclusionary era." —New York University professor Dr. Jeffrey Sammons

The United Golfers Association and other predominantly black organizations could not have existed if there hadn't been facilities available to people of color. Before World War II, African-Americans were denied access to most municipal courses and private clubs. In 1939, there were 5,209 golf facilities in the United States. More than 3,000 of them were private, 1,200 daily fee and 700 municipally owned. Fewer than 20 were open to blacks and most of those were located either in the North or Midwest as evidenced by the various UGA national championship venues. The UGA took its annual showcase event to Sunset Hills near Kankakee, Ill., Douglass Park in Indianapolis, Rackham in Detroit, Mohansic in New York, Highland Park in Cleveland, Cobbs Creek in Philadelphia and Palos Park in Chicago. The Casa Loma Country Club at Powers Lake, Wis., a nine-hole course with cottages and a pristine lake, was perhaps the most lavish venue. All were daily-fee courses with diverse populations.

Although the public golf course has served as the primary avenue to the game for African-Americans, black-owned private country clubs such as Shady Rest and Mapledale set a standard of self-reliance in the 1920s that resonated into the 1990s. Theirs is a story of independence emulated years later by African-American families in Ohio and North Carolina. The greater purpose has always been securing a place in the game, and access has forever been an issue. Like the civil rights movement of the 1960s, golf's freedom was secured on small battlefields, none more important than at Langston Golf Course in Washington, D.C. Just as Shady Rest and Mapledale provide a backdrop for African-Americans' attempt at ownership, Langston symbolizes integration of America's public facilities. Both avenues converged in concert, although of the more than 16,000 public and private golf courses in the United States in 1999, only four were owned by African-

The original Shady Rest Country Club logo.

Shady Rest Country Club, one of the first black-owned golf clubs in the United States.

The clubhouse and practice putting green at Shady Rest Country Club.

Americans. The history of those four, however, and their predecessors is significant in the overall progression of the game among people of color.

To fully appreciate the successes of African-Americans in establishing even the smallest foothold in golf, it is necessary to adequately depict the force of their staunchest foe. The role of segregation in denying them access to the game can not be overstated. "We couldn't play the course and my Daddy was the greens superintendent there and we lived on the golf course," said former PGA Tour player Charlie Owens of Winter Haven (Fla.) CC, where he caddied in the 1930s and '40s. "Hell, a black man couldn't play anywhere in Florida in those days and not many places anywhere in this entire country." If African-Americans were going to scale the fence to athletic and social freedom, they would have to do it on their own, and most assuredly, against all odds.

Aspiring African-American golfers fought the system through acuity rather than prideful arrogance. Instead of storming the clubhouses of America and demanding equal access to the golf course, most patiently waited in the wings for the right opening. A few purchased their own playground. An opportunity for self-reliance arose in September 1921, when the African-American-owned Progressive Realty Company of Westfield, N.J., purchased the previously segregated Westfield Golf Club. The centerpiece of 31 acres of land, Westfield offered all the amenities of a true country club, including six tennis courts, a croquet area, bridle paths, facilities for trap shooting and a nine-hole golf course. Located in the shadow of New York City along the Westfield-Scotch Plains border, the club became Shady Rest and African-American golfers had their first real home.

From the beginning, Shady Rest brought African-Americans together in harmony and accord. There were no social

> Shady Rest was an overground railroad to freedom of lifestyle and expression. Once loosed, African-Americans would fight never again to be harnessed by society's yoke.

Wide, broad fairways characterize the Shady Rest golf course.

boundaries. Businessmen and porters were equals on the club's membership roll. Their wives sat on the wide verandas in the cool evenings and engaged in lively conversation while their children chased fireflies. Soft music and the intoxicating smell of baked ham emanated from the restaurant. It was, as club president B.C. Gordon noted, "an atmosphere among refined ladies and gentlemen."

Unanimity gave way to discord as Shady Rest—as most country clubs do—suffered through some early growing pains. In 1925, self-serving factions from New Jersey and New York engaged in a tug-of-war for control of Shady Rest. The New York contingent, headed by Henry Parker, eventually rose to power but was forced to relinquish it after Parker and another member allegedly absconded with the club's mortgage payment. William Willis Sr., who ran a successful taxi cab company,

John Shippen, the first African-American to play in the U.S. Open, served as Shady Rest's head pro and greenskeeper for more than 30 years.

rescued the club from financial straits after the New Yorkers were deposed. Under his guidance, Shady Rest became a haven for black golfers on the East Coast and a favorite stop for some of the country's top black entertainers. The club was also a magnet for scholars and social reformers such as W.E.B. DuBois. Shady Rest was an above-ground railroad to freedom of lifestyle and expression. Once loosed, African-Americans would fight never again to be harnessed by society's yoke.

John Shippen came to Shady Rest in 1932 as its superintendent and professional, further enhancing his role as the most prominent African-American golfer of the pre-World War II era, and served as the club's rock through shifting tides. He endeared himself to the community and club members, but ultimately even he could not save Shady Rest from being ceded to the township of Scotch Plains in 1963. The next year Shady Rest became the Scotch Hills Country Club and opened to the public. Shady Rest will forever occupy a seat in history as the birthplace of African-Americans' golfing independence. The club fostered an environment some historians believe will never be equaled. Said Dr. Jeffrey Sammons of New York University, "We tend to think of integration in positive terms. But new generations will not have the kind of rapport, relationship, endearment to a black institution as would those who came up in a segregated, exclusionary era."

Nevertheless, Shady Rest planted the seed of ownership and soon other African-Americans followed the example set by its founders. In 1926, entrepreneur Robert H. Hawkins put together $6,000 and assumed a pre-existing $10,000 mortgage in purchasing the 190-acre former estate of Dr. John Witt Randall in Stow, Mass. He established the Mapledale Country Club on the property, complete with clubhouse, tennis courts and a nine-hole golf course. Located about 25 miles west of Boston, Mapledale was constructed for the enjoyment of locals but gained prominence nationally by hosting the UGA championship several times. The club catered to the upwardly mobile as well as the blue-collar worker. One newspaper article depicted the club's early success: "On holidays and weekends may be seen from 50 to 200 machines, ranging from Fords to Packards, parked at this club." However, Hawkins couldn't keep the club afloat financially and was forced to relinquish all but a small interest in it. In 1929, Mapledale became Stow Golf and Country Club, a public facility which blacks still frequented but could no longer call their own. The property was later sold at auction.

> Most of the early African-American country clubs had short life spans mainly due to a lack of financial support from the black community and the economic hardships of the Depression.

Nowhere was segregation more of a hindrance to the evolution of golf in this country than in the nation's capital. In the early '20s, the District's parks and public buildings were ruled by a close-minded North Carolinian named Lieut. Col. Clarence O. Sherrill, who sought to snuff out growing interest in the game by African-Americans by instituting a segregation policy at city-owned courses. By his decree, blacks were allowed to play the East Potomac course exclusively after 3 p.m. each Tuesday and the three-hole West Potomac Park course after noon on Wednesdays. Whites were barred from playing those courses during Sherrill's imposed blackout.

Black-owned private country clubs such as Shady Rest and

Courtesy: Larry Londino/Montclair State University

(Left and right) Photographic stills made from an 8mm home movie taken at the old Shady Rest.

Mapledale were a rarity. Most courses with a large number of African-American players were the result of city officials' determination to keep the races separated. In 1925, D.C. leaders graciously conceded a poorly maintained par-3 course adjacent to Lincoln Memorial for the primary use of blacks. This kind of generosity was practiced in many of the country's major metropolitan areas heavily populated by African-American golf enthusiasts. Despite course conditions so inferior they were assailed in the black media, many of the era's top black golfers developed their skills at such facilities. The shaggy layouts placed a premium on creativity and imagination but further distanced the African-American golfer from his white counterpart.

Compliments of Henry Stone

Howard Wheeler at Cobbs Creek in 1951.

Blacks still aspired to own golf courses and there were limited opportunities during this period. One presented itself in 1926 when a D.C. group led by real estate dealer Victor R. Daly purchased 23 acres in suburban Maryland. The National Capital Country Club officially opened in May of 1927. The grass was sparse in spots on the short course, thus delaying its opening until July. So, instead of a golf tournament on that beautiful spring day, the club was christened by the annual Howard University track and field meet.

Other attempts by African-Americans to own and develop private country clubs in the 1920s included the Booker T. Washington CC in Buckingham, Pa., and the Acorn CC outside Richmond, Va. In 1930, a group of African-American businessmen in Los Angeles purchased the Parkridge Country Club in southern California. The property had among its 650 acres an 18-hole golf course and dozens of small, furnished bungalows for what might

have been the first black-owned golf resort with private housing.

Most of the early African-American country clubs had short life spans mainly due to a lack of financial support from the black community and the economic hardships of the Depression. They often disappeared from the radar screen without public notice. Those that survived, such as Clearview Golf Course in East Canton, Ohio, and Freeway Golf Course outside Philadelphia, were sustained by individuals whose spirit would not

*The 11th green at the **Clearview Golf Course** in East Canton, Ohio.*

be broken by any amount of adversity.

William J. and Marcella Powell were two of them. Powell grew up in Minerva, Ohio, a small Midwestern town with only one black family—the Powells. William was exposed to the game by a white doctor for whom he started caddieing when he was only nine years old. Later he captained the Minerva High School golf and football teams. His love for golf followed him into the military service during World War II, but, like many other African-American servicemen who served their country only to find little if any reciprocity upon discharge, Powell discovered few open doors to the game when he returned to Stark County. However, he convinced two black physician friends to partner

On October 10, 1996, exactly a week after Tiger Woods made the Las Vegas Invitational his first PGA Tour victory, Bull Creek opened with free rounds to the public.

Warren Massenburg.

with him in construction of a vision. With their investment and what meager earnings he could spare from employment at a roller bearing factory, Powell purchased a small fruit farm. He and his wife, Marcella, worked tirelessly developing the property. They planted most of the trees by hand and the grass seeds while walking with a hand spreader. "When a tree died," Powell said, "it was like losing a member of the family." In the spring of 1948, the Powells opened nine holes, making them the first African-Americans to design, build, own and operate a golf course in the United States. They eventually bought out their partners and, in the 1970s, expanded the course to 18 holes. Said Powell, "I could have done anything to take care of my family. I chose this and stuck with it. That was all. I'm not a quitter."

Neither were the founding members of the Greater Philadelphia Golf and Country Club, who masterminded the purchase of Turnersville Golf Course in Sicklerville, N.J., in 1967. The founders—Maxwell Stanford, Albert Letson, Robert Salisbury and J. Lester Blocker—changed the name of the 18-hole course to Freeway and opened it to daily-fee play a year later. Operated by a black board of directors, Freeway hosted the 43rd United Golfers Association National Championship in 1969. Its head pro, Bill Bishop, and several members, including Jimmy Wilburn and Robert Miller, are former UGA standouts. The annual Bill Bishop Open still attracts top African-American play-

Samuel Solomon.

ers from around the country.

North Carolina, historically one of the South's most dogged disciples of segregation, is home to one of the oldest black-owned courses, Meadowbrook CC—and one of its newest, Bull Creek G&CC. Meadowbrook, a nine-holer in the Raleigh suburb of Garner, was developed from 140 acres of tobacco farmland bought in 1958 by businessmen M. Grant Batey, James Joseph Sansom Jr. and Paul Jervay. It was a private club with more than 150 members before a turn in financial fortunes forced its owners to downgrade to semi-private status. "A lot of people said it wasn't going to work," said Batey, the club's executive vice president and lone survivor among its founding fathers. "But we were determined and struggled on."

*The 221-yard par-three 13th hole under construction at **Bull Creek**.*

Their Carolina neighbors at Bull Creek, in Louisburg, were just as tenacious, especially after two of them, Samuel Solomon and Zollie Gill, visited Meadowbrook in 1992 on a fact-finding mission. What they discovered was slightly unsettling. "I was discouraged by what they told us," said Gill. "But Sam was persistent, and it's a good thing he was. We found out that we didn't need all the permits in this county to build a golf course that they needed at Meadowbrook." They still had to sell the idea of turning 170 acres of prime farmland, most of which was owned by family patriarch Warren E. Massenburg, into a golf course. As Massenburg's nephew, Gill had a certain amount of influence. Solomon, a relative by marriage, was the resident golf enthusiast. The two of them convinced Massenburg, an astute businessman who had made a small fortune in rest homes for the disabled and elderly, that a golf course would not only be a financial success but another chapter in Massenburg's legacy in Granville and Franklin counties. In the spring of 1994, they broke ground.

Solomon and Gill, both of whom grew up as farm hands, used their knowledge about

*The completed 13th hole at **Bull Creek**.*

irrigation systems and agronomy in overseeing the project. With private funding and a bank loan on the property, the group hired a Raleigh-based golf course architecture firm to design the initial nine holes and a small construction company to clear the land. "I had more equipment than the first contractor," said Massenburg of the low-budget operation (compared to today's multi-million dollar golf course developments). "I own seven tractors myself."

For every success story there are dozens of tales of disappointment scattered along African-Americans' path to access any golf facility in the United States.

On October 10, 1996, exactly a week after Tiger Woods made the Las Vegas Invitational his first PGA Tour victory, Bull Creek opened with free rounds to the public. Franklin County elite and public officials attended the opening ceremonies covered by the local media. In the fall of 1998, the club opened its back nine. Said Massenburg, "Plenty of people said when we broke ground it would never happen. But we've had at least 150 people out there playing in one day. I feel real good over some of the things I've done in my life. This golf course is certainly one of them."

Nearly 60 years earlier, in 1939, another public course constructed specifically for people of color opened in the nation's capital. Langston Golf Course, described as "modern in every respect," brought to fruition the efforts of several groups, including the Royal Golf Club and Wake Robin Golf Club, to develop an accessible facility of merit in the District. Prior to Langston's opening, the two black golf organizations and other D.C. golf enthusiasts had been forced, because of Lt. Col. Sherrill's "efforts," to travel as far as New York to play an 18-hole golf course. And although only nine holes of the new layout were displayed on that June morning, Langston was considered a significant coup for those dedicated to making the game accessible to everyone.

Named in honor of John Mercer Langston, the first person of color from Virginia to serve in the U.S. House of Representatives (in the late 1800s), the course was in far from stellar condition on opening day. Some of the greens were patchy and a few holes were so poorly designed that they were later rerouted. Still, Langston was a salve to the wounds of District golfers who had been denied access for so long. East Potomac's white populace might have been the worst offender. Two years after Langston's opening, a group of

Virginia Historical Society

John Mercer Langston, the first African-American elected to Congress from Virginia. The first golf course for people of color in Washington, D.C. was named after Langston.

golfers led by Royal Golf Club members Edgar G. Brown and Dr. George Adams sought to play East Potomac. After being attacked by rock-throwing whites, the group took their plight to noted politician Harold Ickes, then Secretary of the Interior. Forced to re-examine the discriminatory policies prevalent at East Potomac and the District's other public facilities, Ickes declared, "They are taxpayers, they are citizens, and they have a right to play golf on public courses on the same basis as whites."

Ickes' position notwithstanding, few public officials attacked the blatant bigotry faced by blacks in their struggle to integrate the game and the harassment by whites remained rampant. It wasn't until the mid-'50s, when Langston expanded to 18 holes, that Sherrill's policy was struck down, and blacks were finally allowed to play all of the District's public facilities. Langston eventually became a first-rate facility frequented by blacks from all walks of life. It hosted the Capital City Open, one of the UGA's premier events, and served as a training ground for some of the country's top African-American players, including Lee Elder. From the ashes of segregation arose a public facility of equal access and a beacon of hope for African-American golfers everywhere.

Harold Ickes, who, as Secretary of the Interior under Franklin Roosevelt, ordered Washington, D.C.'s, public courses to integrate.

For every success story there are dozens of tales of disappointment scattered along African-Americans' path to access any golf facility in the United States. Public attention was focused squarely on the plight of people of color to gain equality in golf by the Shoal Creek scandal in 1990 when a Southern autocrat named Hall Thompson admitted his club had no black members (and no plans to ever admit any) because that "just wasn't done in Birmingham." His comments incurred the wrath of civil rights activists and, subsequently, golf's watchdogs. As a result of the Shoal Creek incident, exclusionary practices long prevalent at many private clubs in this country were exposed and blacks given new choices. Two years after Shoal Creek, 17 percent of the estimated 495,000 African-American golfers (about the same percentage of Caucasian golfers) claimed to have played most of their rounds at private country clubs. The figures suggest increased access and exposure to quality facilities for an emerging African-American golfing populace. If that is indeed the case, it all started with a desire for self-reliance and a determination to own a piece of America.

CHAPTER 6

SOUL MATES AND SOLE SURVIVORS

"My style of play was aggressive, dynamic and mean."
—Althea Gibson

The wounds inflicted by Ohio State University's Scarlet Course and the pressure of contending for a national championship required more than a Band-Aid. The UCLA Bruins needed emergency surgery to stitch up shaken confidence and sagging hopes amid the lengthening shadows of a once-in-a-lifetime shot at collegiate history. However, a meeting of the minds and a serious heart check would have to suffice. A traffic jam at the 17th hole gave the UCLA contingent an opportunity to assess the situation. During the 11th-hour conference, the Bruins quickly calculated they were six shots down to rival San Jose State. "We are not going to lose," LaRee Pearl Sugg, the team's lone African-American player, said emphatically to her teammates. "We still have a chance. We can do it."

LaRee Pearl Sugg.

Four holes earlier, it was Sugg who needed a pep talk. She had inadvertently hit her tee shot from a few inches in front of the tee markers, thus incurring a two-shot penalty, which resulted in a double bogey at the par-3. Although Sugg rallied with consecutive birdies, she felt personally responsible for her team's slide and desperately sought to make amends. The opportunity came on the first hole of a sudden-death playoff after a combination of UCLA birdies and SJSU lapses gave the Bruins a reprieve. "I had a chance to go from goat to hero," said Sugg, reliving her defining moment on that May afternoon in 1991. She holed a 25-foot birdie putt in the play-off to lift UCLA to the national championship and become the first African-American female member of an NCAA championship winning golf team. "It will forever be my proudest moment," she said.

Sugg might never have received an opportunity to bask in the national spotlight if not for the perseverance of some formidable predecessors in the struggle to level the playing field for people of color. Strong, unyielding, heroic women such as Ann Gregory, Paris Brown, Maggie Hathaway, Althea Gibson, Renee Powell and Barbara Douglas made immeasurable contributions toward the evolution of the game among African-Americans. Their stories bespeak a softer yet equally passionate desire to stake out a place in golf, by a group that possessed half the clout of their male counterparts yet faced twice the number of obstacles.

Althea Gibson.

African-American women have displayed amazing strength and resilience in the face of discrimination on both the political and social fronts in this country. These golf enthusiasts were not only thwarted by the same forces of racism outside their community that blocked all African-Americans' access to the game, but also by male chauvinism within it. The UGA had allowed female players to participate in its National Open as early as 1930, but it was not until nine years later that women were allowed to join the organization.

> At the zenith of her career, Gregory was considered the country's best African-American player. The UGA titles were a testament to her skill, but they hardly quelled her desire for universal acceptance.

During that early period, African-American women's golf was dominated by Lucy Williams of Indianapolis and Marie Thompson of Chicago. They won the UGA national amateur six times between them from 1930-1946. Another prominent player was Julia Towns Siler of St. Louis, who was credited with more than 100 victories during an illustrious amateur career. Mrs. Siler and her husband, George, were charter members of the Atwater Golf Club, founded in 1919 by St. Louis' upwardly mobile African-Americans. The black press dubbed them the "King and Queen of St. Louis Golf." Other accomplished players of this generation included Chicagoans Ella Able, Melanie Moye, Thelma Cowans (a fierce competitor who captured the UGA national title four times from 1947-1955) and Geneva Wilson. In 1944, maverick tournament promoter George S. May invited Wilson to play in his prestigious All-American Open at Tam O'Shanter Golf Club in Chicago, making her the first African-American woman to compete in the event.

Ann Gregory participating in a golf demonstration at Gleason Park in Gary, Ind.

Although specific details about the competition among African-American women are sketchy, some exceptional players were developed on those UGA battlegrounds. One of them, Ann Moore Gregory, a Gary, Ind., housewife by way of Aberdeen, Miss., proved her game was good enough to cross racial lines and hurdle national boundaries. Born in the underbelly of the South on July 25, 1912, Ann was orphaned at the age of four when her parents were killed in an automobile accident. Raised in an orphanage, she was eventually sent to the home of a white family named Sanders, who gave her room and board in return for her service as a domestic. Her "escape" to Indiana came 22 years later, when she married Percy Leroy Gregory and bid farewell to a maid uniform. Her employers were less than thrilled about her emancipation. Recollected the typically outspoken Gregory in *The Illustrated History of Women's Golf,* "(They) cried like babies. They said people in the North were so cold and that I didn't deserve being treated like that. I said, 'Mrs. Sanders, you've prepared me very well for mistreatment.'"

The first sport Gregory took up was not golf, but tennis, and she proved a natural athlete. Within a few years of moving to Gary, she became proficient enough at the game to win the city championship. She didn't take up golf until 1943, while Percy was in the middle of a stint in the armed forces. Ann joined the Chicago Women's Golf Association, an organization formed in 1937 by a group of black women led by Anna Mae Robinson. Under the tutelage of UGA stalwart Calvin Ingram, Ann's game developed so rapidly that by 1947 she had won several local and regional championships, including the Joe Louis Invitational. Gregory received a late-summer invitation to play in the Tam O'Shanter (following in Wilson's footsteps) and her first opportunity to see how her game measured up against the country's best women golfers. It didn't. Like most of the top African-American players, Ann could consistently shoot in the low- to mid-70s on municipal tracks but had difficulty meeting the challenges of a championship course the caliber of Tam O'Shanter.

Her disappointing showing only inspired Gregory to work more diligently on her game. In 1950, the extra effort paid off when she won the first of her four UGA championships. At the zenith of her career, Gregory was considered the country's best African-American player. The UGA titles were a testament to her skill, but they hardly quelled her desire for universal acceptance. Dogged by her less than stellar performance in the All-American Open, Ann sought redemption. Her opportunity came in September of 1956 when she became the first African-American to enter the U.S. Women's Amateur, contested that year at Meridian Hills CC in Indianapolis. There, her first opponent was heralded

*A great champion, **Ann Gregory** won more than 200 golf trophies in her long career. She is shown here in 1966.*

white golfer Caroline Cudone.

No first-round match in the 61-year history of the event had ever generated so much attention. Media from across the country swarmed the first tee and elbowed for space among the curious gallery members. Gregory put on a powerful performance, often leaving her opponent in awe. Later, Cudone would tell reporters, "Her game was scaring me to death. Her shots were so long. Ann came closer to more holes-in-one than just about anyone I can remember. It always seemed she was knocking it three feet from the cup." However, Cudone was every bit Gregory's equal and when the latter faltered down the stretch, Cudone escaped with a 2-and-1 victory. (Marlene Stewart would eventually win the championship, beating a young phenom named JoAnne Gunderson in the final.)

Gregory used that USGA experience as a confirmation of her ability and a springboard to national notoriety and fame. She would play in several more U.S. Amateurs, recording her best finish in the 1959 event at Congressional Country Club in Bethesda, Md., where she advanced to the third round before being eliminated by Diana Hoke. Gregory's unbridled passion for golf was only surpassed by her hatred of racism. Indeed, her most significant contribution to the game might have been as a civil rights activist in the early '60s. Her home course in Gary, a municipal facility called Gleason Park, consisted of a well-manicured 18-hole course reserved for white golfers, and an unkempt nine-holer used by blacks—at least until Gregory grew tired of the arrangement and decided to make a statement of her own. "My tax dollars are taking care of the big course," she declared, "and there's no way you can bar me from it." She played the 18-hole course unbothered, forever shattering segregation at Gleason Park.

Gregory would win her last UGA Championship in 1966, at the age of 54. Despite encouragement from fellow competitors and potential financial backers to turn professional, Gregory remained active in amateur golf well into her 70s. In 1989, still mourning her husband's death earlier that year, she won the golf competition at the U.S. National Senior Olympics. It was her last championship. She died of complications from a respiratory infection on Feb. 5, 1990. She was eulogized as a breath of fresh air and an inspiration to golfers and anyone else who might otherwise have been afraid to face new frontiers.

During her long, illustrious career, Gregory crossed paths with a number of other African-American women who may never have seen themselves as pioneers but were nonetheless instru-

> "My tax dollars are taking care of the big course … and there's no way you can bar me from it."
> — Ann Gregory
>
> She played the 18-hole course unbothered, forever shattering segregation at Gleason Park.

mental in breaking down barriers of gender and race. Some of them were members of a Washington D.C.-based group called the Wake-Robin Golf Club. The club was founded April 22, 1937, during a party at the Washington, D.C., home of Helen Webb Harris, an educator and wife of a prominent D.C. doctor. The club's purpose was described simply and eloquently in this 1985 letter to the membership from charter member Ethel Williams: "The foremost aim of the club was and continues to be to perpetuate golf among Negro women, to make potential players into champions and to make a permanent place for Negro women in the world of golf." The club succeeded in many areas, including leading the fight against segregation at municipal courses in the District. Several members joined their husbands, who belonged to the Royal Golf Club, in persuading city officials to turn an old city trash dump into Langston Golf Course. The Wake-Robin, which derived its name from the purplish wild flower that thrived in the Middle Atlantic states, also produced champion golfers. None was more accomplished than Ethel Funches, a D.C. transplant from South Carolina, who won an unprecedented five UGA national amateur titles from 1959-1973. Funches captured numerous inter-club championships and in the process earned a reputation as one of the UGA's grittiest competitors. However, as was common during that period, her comfort zone did not extend beyond the primarily black golf circuit. Consequently, though she was a legend at obscure stops along golf's back roads, Funches remains largely unknown at the national level.

While women such as Gregory and Funches fought the system by organizing clubs and confronting social injustice, Paris Brown made her mark within the system, instilling African-American women golfers with a combin- ation of knowl- edge of the rules and pro- tocol. A former census taker, Brown

*The **Wake Robin Golf Club**, an all-female, all-black, golf club, founded in 1937. The club still exists to this day.*

rose rapidly through the administrative ranks of the Wake-Robin Club and then the UGA, becoming in 1954 the organization's first female national tournament director and one of its most influential ambassadors. Brown provided stability and uniformity for the

UGA and drafted a strict set of rules applicable to all UGA affiliates. "Paris worked tirelessly to make sure things ran smoothly and she commanded a lot of respect," recalled Timothy Thomas, long-time first-tee announcer at UGA events and Brown's successor as tournament director in 1964. "She had a way of putting people in their place nicely but firmly. It was remarkable because she had no prior experience running professional golf tournaments."

> African-American women made incremental strides in amateur golf and served the UGA in various capacities …

Brown, who cut a tall, stately figure among her golfing contemporaries, learned on the job. Her insistence that UGA tournaments be conducted with the same kind of integrity as PGA Tour events and her refusal to let anything or anyone —especially gamblers — taint one of her tournaments was a source of pride to most UGA members and an irritation to some. She had numerous clashes with males who challenged her authority. She was unwavering in her sense of justice and devotion to fair play. A player discovered wagering during a UGA tournament was immediately disqualified. Throughout her career, Brown championed causes critical to minority access and exposure. Her efforts did not go unnoticed. "Paris was a wonderful woman who deserved accolades," said Philadelphia's Phyllis Meekins, who served as handicap chairman of the Eastern Golf Association, a UGA satellite that hosted a testimonial dinner for Brown in the mid-'70s. Among the tributes to Brown was a congratulatory letter from PGA commissioner Joseph C. Dey Jr., acknowledging her many years of service to the game. African-American golf lost one of its most dedicated patrons when Paris Brown succumbed to a lengthy illness in 1990.

Paris Brown has been called the Godmother of black golf.

Phyllis Meekins.

African-American women made incremental strides in amateur golf and served the UGA in various capacities, as trailblazing male pros such as Bill Spiller and Charlie Sifford broke down barriers. However, it took a female national hero of another sport to finally crash the color barrier in the women's pro ranks. In 1963, tennis legend Althea Gibson became the first black member of the Ladies Professional Golf Association. "I was always a competitor, but being a competitor, I've always wanted to win," said Gibson in a 1998 biodocumentary. "I always played to win by using my God-given skills." Those skills were considerable, as was her desire to rise above meager beginnings.

Althea was born Aug. 25, 1927, in Silver, S.C.,

the daughter of sharecroppers Daniel and Annie Gibson. At the age of three and already showing signs of being a tomboy, she was sent by her parents to New York City to live with an aunt who resided in the Bronx at 143rd Street between Lenox and Seventh avenues. It was a tough neighborhood ruled by various social outcasts and the truculent and combative Althea could easily have become a product of her environment if not for an incandescent athleticism that eventually caught the attention of one savior after another. The first to come to her rescue was a ten-

Althea Gibson. After winning the U.S. Open and Wimbledon tennis crowns, she took up golf and eventually competed on the LPGA Tour.

nis enthusiast named Buddy Walker, who took one look at the prowess with which Gibson played paddle tennis in the street outside her stoop and decided there was no limit to her potential. He introduced her to lawn tennis at the Harlem River courts in 1941 and she thrived under the direction of Fred Johnson, the tennis pro at the all-black Cosmopolitan Tennis Club. "My style of play was aggressive, dynamic and mean," Gibson declared in the documentary.

Later, Gibson met boxing champion Sugar Ray Robinson, who owned a supper club in Harlem. He convinced the high school dropout to complete her education. At the age of 21, she graduated from a Wilmington, N.C., high school and headed to Florida A&M University on a tennis scholarship. By 1950, Gibson had established herself as the top player in the American Tennis Association, a black organization that existed in the shadow of the segregated United States Lawn Tennis Association. That same year she became the first African-American woman to compete in a USLTA national event. It was a mere stepping stone to international stardom. By 1958 the tall, slender, young woman had won a collection of Grand Slam titles, including consecutive Wimbledon and U.S. Open crowns, collected two Female Athlete of the Year awards, been feted with a ticker tape parade in New York and retired as a tennis icon.

Althea hard at work on the practice tee.

Gibson constantly sought new challenges and excelled at just about every endeavor she attempted. She became a jazz saxophonist and singer, cutting a modestly successful record titled "So

Much to Live For." By the early '60s, she had toured as a member of the Harlem Globetrotters, appeared as a soloist on the Ed Sullivan Show and landed a bit part in a John Wayne movie. But it wasn't celebrity she craved most—it was competition.

> Gibson was the classic big-hitter who struggled around the greens.

Introduced to golf, she quickly transformed an abundance of raw talent into enough skill to turn professional. Gary Volpe, owner and head professional at Englewood CC in New Jersey, graciously extended an invitation to Gibson to practice at his course and become an honorary member. In 1963, she headed out on tour. The uncharted waters of the LPGA might have drowned one less buoyant and confident than she. On more than one occasion, Gibson had to change her shoes in her car at tournament sites because she wasn't allowed in the clubhouse. At other tournaments, she was barred from playing altogether. Said Renee Powell, who became the second African-American member of the LPGA in 1967, "Lots of tournaments were called invitationals, [which meant] they could invite everybody on the tour or not invite anybody they didn't want to. And they didn't have to invite Althea."

In October 1965, Gibson married longtime beau Will Darben. Marital bliss and security helped her withstand some of the abuses she faced during the early part of her pro golf career. So did her personality, which had grown less combative with maturity. She would often hide the pain of a slight through levity. Others ran interference for her, including then-LPGA tournament director Lenny Wirtz, whom Powell credits with leading a stand against discrimination. "They simply said, 'We won't play in cities where everyone can't play'," Powell said.

Gibson was the classic big-hitter who struggled around the greens. Consequently, she never had a breakthrough season. Said former LPGA star and television analyst Judy Rankin, "She might have been a real player of conse-

(Above and at right) Althea sometimes struggled on and around the greens.

quence had she started when she was young. She was an athlete not unlike Babe (Zaharias). She came along during a difficult time in golf, gained the support of a lot of people and quietly made a difference." From 1963-1977, Gibson played in 171 LPGA events and the closest she came to victory was a three-way playoff in the 1970 Immke Buick Open in Columbus, Ohio. She posted a 75.82 scoring average in 1967, her most lucrative ($5,567) year as a professional. The numbers fail to show how well she acquitted herself on tour. "Althea was a very good player," said Lee Elder, who partnered with Gibson several times. "She could really hit it. She wasn't as complete a player as Renee but she was good."

In 1980, at the age of 53, Gibson attempted a comeback by entering the LPGA Qualifying Tournament, but failed to regain her playing privileges. Except for occasional memorial ceremonies and a few celebrity guest appearances at fund-raisers, she has been a virtual recluse in her East Orange, New Jersey, home in recent years, giving audience only to a shrinking inner circle. "In my opinion, there has never been an athlete or person in this country who has

The strength of Althea Gibson's game was off the tee.

done the things Althea Gibson has," said producer/director Carol Clarke, who befriended Gibson while working on the documentary. "She is the only person to my knowledge who [faced the barriers of discrimination] twice, and she was alone."

During one 1960s trip to the West Coast, Gibson met a diminutive woman named Maggie Hathaway, who was president of the Beverly Hills/Hollywood chapter of the NAACP. Hathaway rivaled the struggling LPGA pro in rebellious spirit, if not athletic accomplishment. "She asked me if we could help get her a sponsor, that she couldn't last much longer on tour if she couldn't get a sponsor," recalled Hathaway. "Unfortunately, we couldn't help her." It was one of the few times Hathaway failed to solicit support for someone in need. Her career is a litany of thorns in the establishment's side.

Hathaway, a native of Shreveport, La., heeded Hollywood's call in 1939 when she and a carload of cousins put the top down on their convertible and sped out of their hometown and headed for Tinsel Town. She landed a job as a soda fountain girl at Price's

Drug Store, where she had heard movie extras hung out. Within weeks, she had gotten her foot into the movie industry's door, working as a movie stand-in for famed black actress Lena Horne. But before long she realized that Jim Crow was as prevalent in California as Louisiana. Said Hathaway, "I go all the way to Hollywood to get away from it and find there is segregation here, too." In the spring of 1946, she and some other black actors picketed the dining room at MGM; when studio officials relented, it meant blacks no longer had to eat at the coffee counter. It marked the beginning of Hathaway's crusade against injustice.

> Hathaway has been first at so many things in her rich life as an actress, journalist, activist and golf instructor.

Nine years later on the eighth tee at Griffith Park Golf Course, heavyweight boxing champion Joe Louis handed her a long iron and told her if she could hit the green on the par-3 he would give her a set of golf clubs. "I had never even swung a golf club before," Hathaway recalled years later, "but I figured I could do better than him [Louis had missed the green with his tee shot] so I accepted the challenge. I hit the worst grass-cutter you ever saw but it made the green. And he bought me the clubs, too." Hathaway became a fair tournament golfer, shooting in the mid-80s on Los Angeles County courses that were open to African-Americans and threatening to picket those that weren't. In the late 1950s, with the help of L.A. county supervisor Kenneth Hahn, she integrated the Western Avenue Women's Golf Club. Her point firmly driven home, Hathaway resigned as a member a month later. "Militant Maggie," as she was known, didn't stop there. In 1960, she organized the Minority Associated Golfers. The group picketed L.A.'s Fox Hills Golf Course until, in 1964, it finally admitted black members. "It wasn't the golf so much that bothered me, it was the color thing," Hathaway said. "I'm part Native American and Afro-American, and I guess my blood just boiled sometimes. I refused to bow down to segregation." Nor would she let others.

Hathaway organized picket lines at PGA tournaments in Southern California and staunchly stood behind Charlie Sifford, Bill Spiller, Teddy Rhodes and others when they set out to break the PGA Tour's color barrier. She wrote columns in several black-owned newspapers condemning the PGA. When Lee Elder qualified for the 1975 Masters, Hathaway applied for media credentials to cover his debut for the *Los Angeles Sentinel*, a black-owned weekly. Masters officials turned down her request. More determined than ever to witness history in person, she obtained credentials through an L.A. radio station. She and Jim Brown, the former professional football player turned actor, flew

*Chester Washington Golf Course manager **David Strider** and **Alan Bennett** lower banners to half mast in memory of former LA County Supervisor Kenneth Hann, who integrated LA County golf courses. **Maggie Hathaway** and **Vera Carter** look on.*

to Atlanta together and then drove on to Augusta. Security stopped the ticket-less Brown at the entrance to Augusta National. "The guy said Jim looked familiar but he couldn't place him," laughed Hathaway. "It was really funny because Jim's face was on a movie marquee right across the street. He was starring in '100 Rifles.'" Famed comedian Jackie Gleason came to the rescue. He convinced the caddiemaster to give Brown a Masters badge in exchange for an autographed picture, and the two hurried to the first tee to witness Elder's opening drive.

(Left to right) **Fred Carter**, **Frank Snow** and **Maggie Hathaway** *share a lighter moment looking at a golf scorecard outside the Chester Washington Golf Course clubhouse.*

"I don't know whether it was exhaustion or excitement, but after Lee hit I fainted right on the spot," recalled Hathaway. "I woke up on a stretcher in the hospital right there at the golf course. I bet I was the first black to be admitted to that hospital."

Hathaway has been first at so many things in her rich life as an actress, journalist, activist and golf instructor. She was a driving force behind the NAACP awards, which eventually developed into the highly acclaimed Image Awards, honoring African-American leaders in arts and entertainment. In 1998, L.A. County officials renamed the Jack Thompson Course in Jesse Owens Park, where Hathaway had taught junior golfers for years, the Maggie Hathaway Par-3 Golf Course. She quietly accepted the honor. "They told me to keep my acceptance speech short," Hathaway said. "So, all I said was, 'I want to thank the board of supervisors and, all power to the people.'"

Renee Powell learned of empowerment about the same time she was memorizing the alphabet. At three, she received a couple of cut-down golf clubs from her father and used them like a skeleton key to unlock every door to the future. Renee's backyard, nine-hole Clearview G&CC, crafted by her father's hands, proved the perfect training ground. Before long the Canton, Ohio, native was pummeling most of the male players who frequented the club. Powell compiled an impressive junior golf record, including UGA national titles in 1959-1961. She also won the Midwest Junior four times, the Sixth City in Cleveland five times and the Northeastern Ohio Junior twice. She was one of the co-favorites in the 1962 U.S. Girls' Junior at the CC of Buffalo in Williamsville, N.Y., but lost to Mary Sawyer in an early match. USGA director Joe Dey was impressed with her skill and placid demeanor. "He was such a warm person," recalled Powell, who also established lifelong friendships with a couple of fellow competitors destined for leadership roles in the USGA. "That's where I met (former USGA president) Judy Bell and (former chairman of the USGA Women's Committee) Barbara McIntire. They were really good players and they treated me very well."

The game both consumed and defined Powell. "There were some people who took it as seriously as I did, but I was very competitive," she said. "I was very shy but very competitive, not to try to beat other people but to beat the game, the course. It was the only sport I played. I practiced constantly." Powell received a scholarship to attend Ohio University but transferred to Ohio State after a year, becoming the team's captain and star. "The natural progression," says Powell, "was to play professionally." She joined Gibson on the LPGA Tour in 1967 and immediately awakened to realities away from her insulated world, enduring daily doses of catcalls, death threats, obscene phone calls and snubs by tournament volunteers. "The players were fine because I grew up with most of them," said Powell. "As for the other stuff, my attitude was you just do what you have to do."

Powell's most frightening moment happened en route to a tournament in Detroit. Outside the airport there appeared to be a full-scale riot in progress. "The National Guard was there and there was a lot of gunfire going on up and down the street," recalled Powell. "It sounded like a combat zone."

> Powell shined more in the roles of ambassador and ground-breaker than playing professional.

Renee Powell, who learned to play on her family's course in Ohio, played the LPGA Tour for 12 years.

Although more accustomed to the friendly fire of competition, she had only minor success in 12 years on tour. She never finished higher than a tie for fourth place (in the Lady Errol Classic in 1972) and earned a career-high $7,840 in 1976. Her scoring average of 75.66 that year was also a career best. Said Rankin, "I don't know how much Renee ever focused on being the best tournament golfer she could be. She seemed to always have a lot of other things going on in her life. And she had a long, loose golf swing that hurt her accuracy at times."

Powell shined more in the roles of ambassador and ground-breaker than playing professional. She toured the Far East for the USO in 1972 and in 1979 became the first woman to serve as a head professional in the United Kingdom, at the Silvermore G&CC in England. She resided in the UK for six years before returning to the states to become the head pro at Seneca GC in Cleveland. After six years there, Powell took over for her father at Clearview, holding membership in both the LPGA and PGA.

Through the Renee Powell/Dupont Pro-Am established in 1986, Powell has supported the Ohio Special Olympics. She also has been instrumental in growing the game throughout the country as a member of the USGA Junior Golf Committee. She received the Dr. Martin Luther King Drum Major for Justice Award in 1991 and the PGA Tour's Card Walker Award in 1997 for contributions to sports overall and golf in particular. One of the first African-Americans groomed for the game almost from the crib, Powell personifies the power of adaptability and being able to work within the system. "Being the first at so many things, I learned that I must be beyond reproach at all times," Powell said. "My upbringing prepared me for most of the challenges. I learned to face [adversity], deal with it and move on."

Renee Powell, with her father, *William*.

Barbara A. Douglas, the first African-American member of the USGA Women's Committee and president/ chief operating officer of the National Minority Golf Foundation, was just being introduced to the game as Powell prepared for a pro career. The Chicago native and former IBM executive—she rose from the ranks of secretary—took up the game in the 1960s after relocating to Toledo, Ohio. Another job transfer sent her to White Plains, N.Y., in the late '70s and that's when she got serious about golf, joining the Blue Hills men's club and becoming a regular member of a Saturday foursome. "They made me play from the men's tees," laughed Douglas. "Nobody wanted to be beaten by Barbara Douglas." Her improving game caught the attention of Blue Hills head pro Jimmy Stewart, who

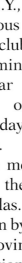

Dara lines up a putt in the Women's Amateur.

Dara Broadus in the 1999 U.S. Women's Amateur.

handed her an application for the U.S. Women's Public Links. Since the qualifying round was only a short drive down the turnpike to Flanders, N.J., Douglas decided to give it a shot. She qualified with an 84 but failed to make match play.

However, the hook was set. She played in several more Public Links before deciding her calling was in golf administration rather than competition. Said Douglas, "I had some wonderful times but I didn't believe I could have a career at IBM and compete in those events. I said, 'Maybe I need to be one of those ladies wearing the blue coats.'" In 1990, she accepted an invitation from USGA Women's Committee Chairman Cora Jane Blanchard to serve on the Public Links committee. Two years later, she was appointed to the women's committee. "I was flabbergasted," said Douglas, who was selected to chair the Public Links committee in 1999.

> "Sometimes I put too much pressure on myself because I care so much about women's golf and making the game better for everyone."
>
> — LaRee Pearl Sugg

With only one minority among the 140 qualifiers for the 1998 Women's Public Links, Douglas is transfixed on bridging the gap between good intentions and the first tee. As a member of the USGA's strategic planning committee, she urged the group to focus more on the grass-roots golfer than his country-club counterpart, and to reach out to the masses rather than to a few. Of greater concern to Douglas, however, is the place of African-Americans in golf's manufacturing arena and its boardrooms. "I'm more interested in seeing more minority males and females move into the business of golf than into becoming playing professionals," said Douglas, citing one of the NMGF's main objectives. "I push careers in golf. Back at the office there are five jobs on my desk. I'd like to be able to go to our database and find 25 candidates for each of those jobs. One day I will."

Douglas was among the blue-blazered officials at the 1995 U.S. Women's Open at the Broadmoor GC in Colorado Springs, Colo., when LaRee Pearl Sugg stepped back into the national spotlight for the first time since that title-clinching putt in Columbus, Ohio. Her appearance, the first by an African-American in a Women's Open since Powell in the mid-'70s, was heralded by some as a breakthrough for black golfers, one of portent and hope. Sugg saw it as a chance to prove she could play with the best players in the world, in the game's showcase event, and carry the banner of the downtrodden. Said Sugg, "Sometimes I

Barbara Douglas, national competitor, USGA committee member and, since 1999, head of the National Minority Golf Foundation.

put too much pressure on myself because I care so much about women's golf and making the game better for everyone. A lot of times, I let things distract me from my game." Blame it on the microscope effect or a loopy swing not conducive to penal USGA championship layouts—the fact remains that Sugg was not around that Sunday afternoon when a young Swede named Annika Sorenstam captured the first of her consecutive Open crowns. Sugg failed to qualify for the final two rounds, one of the many setbacks in her up-and-down pro career.

But Sugg's "ups" have been memorable. The Petersburg, Va., native was taught the game by her grandfather, Dr. James C. Nelson, a professor and golf coach at Virginia State University. Local professional Russell Pike smoothed the rough edges and before long Sugg became a titan among junior golfers, winning more than 30 titles, qualifying for the LPGA's 1986 UVB Classic as a 16-year-old, and earning an Amy Alcott Scholarship to attend UCLA, where she played a key role on the Bruins' 1991 national championship team. However, the road to the LPGA proved more difficult than she anticipated. After three years of grinding out a living in Europe, Asia and on various domestic mini-tours, Sugg finally earned a tour card in the fall of 1994, becoming only the third African-American member of the LPGA. Keeping it, however, has proven to be a different matter. Since 1996, she has been a conditional player on tour, logging more time in the minor leagues of women's golf than the majors. More discouraging for Sugg is that she hasn't seen many other African-American faces in her rear-view mirror. "It was a long time between Renee and me and there aren't that many coming behind me," she said.

CHAPTER 7

PUBLIC BATTLES, PRIVATE WARS

"He was the ultimate victim in golf." —Bill Spiller Jr., of his father, who helped lead the fight that eventually forced the PGA of America to rescind its Caucasian-only clause.

There have been many soldiers in the battle to gain access to the game. Walter Speedy was one of the first activists. Normally placid Robert (Pat) Ball constantly found himself in the eye of the storm. But perhaps no player was more instrumental in opening up the game to people of color than the relentless Bill Spiller, who spearheaded a rebellion that caused the PGA of America to eventually rescind its Caucasian-only clause. Other civil rights activists such as Alfred (Tup) Holmes and Dr. George C. Simkins Jr. were protagonists in U.S. Supreme Court decisions in the 1950s that impacted play at the grass-roots level. Nearly 40 years later, golf's most influential ruling bodies in this country, the USGA, the PGA Tour and the PGA of America, were forced into the fray by the unfortunate words of a Birmingham (Ala.) zealot named Hall Thompson. Over the years, litigation, perseverance and the growing momentum of social change have gradually opened clubhouse doors to blacks and other minorities. The stories of Spiller, Holmes, Simkins and others engaged in the uphill battle speak volumes about the severity of the incline.

In his autobiography *Just Let Me Play*, Charlie Sifford described Spiller as "the most militant of black golfers." Maggie Hathaway, the scourge of Southern California conformists, said, "The PGA caused Bill Spiller to die with a broken heart." Without question, Spiller fought discrimination in the game on his own terms and ultimately became one of golf's most tragic heroes.

Spiller was more a product of his past than his more famous contemporary Ted Rhodes. Born in 1913 in Tishomingo, Okla., Spiller moved to Tulsa as a nine-year-old to live with his father and quickly learned the drawbacks of being black in America. One day, he went to a store to return some merchandise he had bought. A white sales clerk slapped Bill for what he claimed was impudence. It so angered Bill that he raced home, got a gun, strapped it on and wore it until his sophomore year at Wiley College in Marshall, Texas. "The next guy who puts his hands on me is going to look down this barrel," he recalled in Al Barkow's oral history, *Getting To The Dance Floor*.

Spiller wore his indignation like a polyester leisure suit that was two sizes too small. "He was the angriest person I've ever known because he felt cheated out of an opportunity to play the game," recalled his son, Bill Spiller Jr., a Los Angeles attorney.

Bill Spiller, one of golf's most tragic heroes. Kept off the PGA Tour by the "Caucasian-only" clause, he rarely got the chance to compete against the best players.

He was also an excellent athlete, a two-sport star in high school. However, golf was not one of them. He didn't take up the game in earnest until he was almost 30, but quickly became one of the top black players in Southern California, where he had moved

Without question, Spiller fought discrimination in the game on his own terms and ultimately became one of golf's most tragic heroes.

to live with his mother after earning enough college credits to obtain a teaching certificate in the state of Texas. He pieced together a game based on the swings of his favorite PGA Tour stars. He admired Johnny Bulla's tee ball, Toney Penna's piercing iron shots and Byron Nelson's short but powerful pass. He read the best instruction books, studied every aspect of the game and took pride in being a self-made player. By the mid-1940s, when Spiller met Rhodes, who had accompanied Joe Louis to Los Angeles as the champ's personal golf instructor, Spiller had won several black amateur tournaments in Southern California and felt ready for bigger challenges. He played against the best African-American players in the Joe Louis Invitational at Rackham GC in Detroit and the nation's best pros in the Los Angeles Open and Tam O'Shanter in Chicago, two PGA Tour events open to blacks. He befriended several white players, including Lawson Little, Jimmy Demaret and Bulla, who helped convince Tam O'Shanter CC president George S. May to invite black players to his tournament. In 1947, Spiller turned pro and toured the UGA with Rhodes and Louis, among others. The competition forced him to take a reality check.

Said Spiller in *Getting To The Dance Floor*, "I didn't know there were so many good black players until I went east for the first time. I would tee it up against anybody, and it cost me $1,500 to find out they could play."

Spiller also won his share of matches. One day he hustled Louis out of $7,000 in a showdown that started at dawn and didn't conclude until it was too dark for the pair to see each other. He bought a small house with his winnings. Peace of mind, however, would prove more expensive and elusive. Just as he was offended by the measly salary afforded a freshly minted educator back in Texas and the dime tips he received working as a red cap at the railroad sta-

*Four under par on one hole at Encanto Park in 1952: **Teddy Rhodes**, birdie 3, **Bill Spiller**, birdie 3, **Dr. Lowell Wormsly**, eagle 2 and **Dr. Thomas Crump** par 4.*

Ben Hogan in the rough at the 1948 L.A. Open at Riviera Country Club. Bill Spiller tied Hogan for second place in the first round with a 68.

tion when he first arrived in Los Angeles, he detested restrictions placed on him by other men. His golf intelligence might have soared, but his patience level didn't. Spiller desperately sought to earn a living as a golf professional and that meant eschewing the paltry purses of the black golf tour for the more lucrative PGA circuit. Only one thing stood in his way: the PGA's exclusionary Caucasian-only clause. He felt the sting from the PGA's policies as sharply as that from the white store clerk's hand. He was never shy about letting others know how he felt.

Still, except on rare occasions, Spiller managed to harness his hostility and prove black players belonged beside their white counterparts in professional golf tournaments. He shot a 68 to tie Ben Hogan for second place after the first round of the Los Angeles Open at the Riviera Country Club in 1948. Although he faltered and eventually finished 20 shots behind the victorious Hogan, Spiller finished in the top 60, making him eligible for the next PGA tournament, the Richmond Open outside Oakland. Rhodes also earned an entry into the event, as did another black player, Madison Gunter, in the Monday qualifier. But when they showed up to play, PGA Tour official George Schneiter enforced the Caucasian-only clause and turned them away. However, they refused to go quietly and leaked the story to radio sports commentator Ira Blue of ABC Sports. By nightfall, the entire country knew about the plight of the three black golfers. Next, they hired California attorney John Rowell and announced that they were suing the PGA for $315,000. The tour deflected the

Joe Louis became the first African-American golfer to play in a P.G.A. sanctioned tournament. Joe is shown here with P.G.A. president Horton Smith on the first tee of the San Diego Open, January 17, 1952.

The New York Times

January 16, 1952

P.G.A. Clears Way For Louis To Play

But Ban Continues on Another Negro Entered in San Diego Open Golf Tournament

SAN DIEGO, Calif. Jan. 15 (AP)—The Professional Golfers Association today cleared the way for Joe Louis to play as an invited amateur in the San Diego Open Tournament Thursday.

P.G.A. President Horton Smith said that the organization's by-law ban against non-Caucasians would apply, however, in the case of another Negro, Professional Bill Spiller.

Louis said he would play in the tournament, but that he would continue his fight "to eliminate racial prejudice from golf, the last sport in which it now exists."

Louis thus won the right to play in the tournament—the first Negro ever to do so in a P.G.A. sponsored event—but apparently failed at least for the present in his announced effort to gain equal rights on the links for all Negroes.

Smith explained that Louis' entry was approved as one of ten allowed for invited amateurs exempt from qualification.

He declared the P.G.A. by-law and other qualification rules could not be waived in the case of Spiller except through changes in the P.G.A. constitution. "I am simply applying the rules," he said.

Smith emphasized that the rules would apply to all professionals, including Spiller, and not simply against the Negro.

"But," he added, "Spiller cannot play." He added that aside from the racial issue, Spiller was not an approved P.G.A. professional.

The present controversy started when Louis and Spiller and another Los Angeles professional, Eural Clark, arrived Sunday and were told by the local committee that a nonwhite clause in the P.G.A. contract would bar them.

Louis opened the challenging fight by declaring his aim was to bring the matter into the open and at least put a wedge into the P.G.A. non-Negro rule.

first stone by agreeing to ease restrictions on black players. The tournaments countered by changing their designation from opens to invitationals. This enabled them to continue to discriminate, because invitations were never extended to players of color.

Zeke Hartsfield, Eddie Mallory, Howard Wheeler and Joe Louis at the Coffin Golf Club, Indianapolis, 1948.

It wasn't until four years later that Spiller and his fellow outcasts, led by Louis, were able to deliver the first effective blow to the PGA and its policy. It came at the San Diego Open, where tour officials refused entry to Spiller and another African-American pro named Eural Clark. Louis was allowed to play but only after the PGA was the subject of several critical reports by Walter Winchell in a national radio broadcast that exposed the tour's racial bias even toward a war veteran. At the time, the PGA demonstrated little consistency in classifying its tournaments (some were listed as "sponsored", while others were "co-sponsored") but it has long been held that the champ was the first African-American to play in a PGA "sanctioned" event. Louis' tenacity forced a vote later that week by the PGA Tournament Committee that resulted in a rule change. Essentially, African-Americans could not be kept out of a tournament if they received one of the 10 sponsor exemptions or earned one of 10 spots in the field through open qualifying. However, the association refused to budge on the matter of allowing them to hold PGA Tour membership.

Joe Louis (right) was famous for his boxing exploits, but few people know he was the first African-American to play in a PGA Tour event.

Spiller would play in 10 tour events that year with varying degrees of success and harassment. In Phoenix the week after San Diego, he and six others, including Rhodes, Louis and Charlie Sifford, were in the first two groups to tee off at the start of the tournament. When they arrived at the first hole, according to Sifford's account in *Just Let Me Play*, someone had filled the cup with human excrement. "We held up play half an hour until they took that filthy cup out of the ground and replaced it," wrote Sifford, who also described an awkward scene in which Spiller's insistence on showering in the clubhouse locker room after the round nearly caused a riot.

But the worst of Spiller's fury was reserved for those closest to him. Bill Spiller Jr. was a precocious 13-year-old when he made the mistake of outdriving his father during what was supposed to be a family golf outing. Bill Sr. saw it as a deliberate attempt by a son to upstage, and therefore disrespect, his father. He revoked his son's telephone privileges and confined his activities to the home for a week. "He was just a very competitive man and definitely old school," recalled Bill Jr. "I don't think he had the capacity to understand that you don't teach your children to succeed, then punish them for that success. I never wanted to play golf; I was forced to play. I played out of a sense of fear, mainly." Bill Jr. accused his father of using their golf outings as a means of escaping the house to seek refuge in his favorite bar. Junior left home at 20, did a tour of duty in Vietnam and returned a decorated soldier. He never touched another golf club.

Meanwhile, Spiller's lack of success in the PGA Tour events in which he was allowed to compete (his best finish was a 14th place at the Labatt Open in Canada) forced him to turn to other means of supporting his family. He hustled golf lessons and caddied at Hillcrest Country Club. Said Bill Jr., "That was the most degrading thing that ever happened to him. He had to make a living as a caddie and as a red cap while in his heart he was a golf pro. That hurt him collectively more than anything else. He used to cry about that. He had a burning desire to compete on the tour, [but] he was never able to do that."

Still, Spiller's determination paved the way for others to play. The movement to strike down the PGA's Caucasian-only clause once and for all gained momentum at Hillcrest CC in 1959. The details of what transpired are in dispute. Sifford claims in his book that he initi-

> Still, Spiller's determination paved the way for others to play. The move to strike down the PGA's Caucasian-only clause once and for all gained momentum at Hillcrest Country Club in 1959.

The New York Times

May 18, 1961

P.G.A. Will Shift '62 Tourney Site
Group Removes Event From Los Angeles Because of California's Race Stand

HOLLYWOOD, Fla. May 17 (UPI)—The executive committee of the Professional Golfers Association withdrew its 1962 national championship from Los Angeles for racial reasons today and recommended that the P.G.A. eliminate racial restrictions on membership.

The thirteen-member committee, ending a three-day, mid-year meeting, unanimously passed a resolution to wipe the "Caucasian clause" from the P.G.A. constitution. The resolution will be submitted to the P.G.A.'s annual meeting here Nov. 2-10.

Present P.G.A. regulations limit membership to "professional golfers of the Caucasian race, residing in North or South America."

The resolution came after the committee pulled its 1962 championship out of Los Angeles, apparently as a result of a feud with California Attorney General Stanley Mosk. Mosk said the P.G.A. constitution violates California law because it restricted membership to Caucasians. He said also the tournament could not be played in California if the ranking Negro professional, Charles Sifford, were not allowed to participate.

Tournament Chairman Edwin Carter had explained earlier that Sifford was not eligible to play because he was not a P.G.A. member "and under our constitution, if he were approved today, he could not become a member for at least four years."

Lou Strong, the P.G.A. president, said in announcing the executive committee's action, "Under present conditions in California, the P.G.A. did not feel that it would be possible to conduct a successful tournament of the magnitude of the P.G.A. championship in that state." he said a new site for the tournament would be chosen.

The Los Angeles Junior Chamber of Commerce later announced it would hold a seventy-two-hole Los Angeles open tournament Jan 4-8 in place of the P.G.A. tournament.

ated conversation about the Caucasian-only clause with California Attorney General Stanley Mosk, whom he met at Hillcrest while playing a round with Billy Eckstine. However, Spiller claimed in *Getting To The Dance Floor* that it was he, through a conduit named Harry Braverman, for whom he caddied at Hillcrest, who solicited Mosk's support. Whoever provided the inspiration, the facts are these: Mosk issued a moratorium on the use of California courses by the PGA until it ceased discriminating against non-whites. He also corresponded with other state attorneys general, seeking their assistance in applying pressure on the PGA. The clause was finally removed from the PGA constitution at its annual meeting Nov. 10, 1961, at the Diplomat Hotel in Hollywood, Fla. The Georgia-Alabama delegation co-sponsored the amendment, adopted by a vote of 87-0. Three months prior to that meeting the PGA had moved its 1962 championship, originally scheduled for L.A.'s Brentwood CC, to Aronimink GC in Newtown Square, Pa. Brentwood's Caucasian-only clause violated California law. Through Mosk and his fellow attorneys general, Spiller had forced the PGA of America to fold.

By then, Spiller was well past his prime and engulfed by bitterness. "He didn't believe it was going to do anything to change the situation," said Bill Spiller Jr. "He had been duped many times by then, and, besides, there really weren't many young black golfers around to take advantage of the situation. He was too old and so was Ted Rhodes. There were Sifford and Rafe Botts but not many more of note."

> ... Sifford became the first African-American playing member of the PGA.

Charlie Sifford.

The once promising player also was more than a little ambivalent when, three years later, Sifford became the first African-American playing member of the PGA. "It was dubious to him," allowed Bill Jr., a witness to his father's uncompromising spirit to the bitter end. Confined to a convalescent home after suffering two strokes and being diagnosed with Parkinson's disease, Spiller would clutch the faded newspaper clippings detailing his protests in the clubhouses and exploits on the course. When he died in 1988, those tattered memories were the sum total of his life. Said son of the father, "I see him as forgotten, overlooked and unappreciated; never getting credit for what he actually did."

At least Spiller and other African-American golf enthusiasts could walk onto most municipal courses in Southern California in the 1940s and '50s without fear of being harassed or, even worse, hauled off to jail. Their peers in the country's southern states weren't as fortunate. The emancipation of America's public golf populace began in 1951 when a Georgia doctor, his two sons and a family friend decided to assist the winds of change. It culminated four years later in a Supreme Court decision that shook segregation's foundation and made a folk hero of Alfred (Tup) Holmes in some circles.

(Left to right) C.T. Bell, Alfred (Tup) Holmes and his brother Oliver W. Holmes walk off the 9th hole at North Fulton Golf Course in Atlanta in 1955. They were the first African-American golfers to play on one of Atlanta's heretofore all-white public courses.

The Holmes family was one of prominence in post-war Atlanta. Dr. Hamilton M. Holmes Sr. conducted his family practice out of an office on famed Auburn Ave. in the heart of the city. His son, Oliver Wendell Holmes, was a well-respected minister and a conservative by nature. Tup was the outspoken sibling, a radical who loved to stir the drink long before it was fashionable. He had learned to play golf as a teenager and competed for the Tuskegee Institute team in the late 1930s. He served as union steward at Lockheed Aircraft in Marietta, Ga., in 1951, when the Holmes trio joined Charles T. Bell to make a stand against segregation.

This foursome shared a passion for golf and, like most of Atlanta's African-American elite, they all belonged to black-owned and black-run Lincoln Country Club, a nine-hole layout better known for the quality of its buffet than its course conditions. "If you weren't seen at Lincoln on the weekends, you weren't part of the in-crowd," recalled Bell, whose family owned a real estate company on Auburn Ave. "The course, though, was not in good shape. The greens looked like someone had taken a lawn mower, cut an area and put some sand on it. Most of us were former caddies, so we knew how a golf course should look. We became discontented and went to the board of directors seeking improvements." When the board refused to take action, about 20 members, including the Holmeses and Bell, united and began to meet regularly in Bell's office. In one of those meetings, Tup issued a challenge. "He said, 'To hell with trying to get them to fix up Lincoln. Let's go and play Bobby Jones.'"

Some in attendance nearly choked on the suggestion.

Although Bobby Jones Golf Course, located on the affluent northwest side of town, was one of seven public venues within the city limits, it was off limits to African-Americans unless they happened to be carrying someone else's golf clubs. Sensing resistance to the idea, Tup and Bell came up with a plan to help persuade the others.

In August 1954, U.S. District Judge T. M. Kennerly decreed that blacks had a right to play golf on municipal courses by virtue of a prior ordinance abolishing segregation on Houston's public courses.

They would dispatch ahead one of their members, Kusuth B. Hill, whose blond hair and fair complexion had enabled him to pass for Caucasian on several ruses, to infiltrate the whites-only course. "We had played similar tricks many times," laughed Bell. However, the racism with which he and the Holmeses were confronted on that mid-summer morning was no laughing matter. "The head pro told us straight out we couldn't play, that they didn't allow no niggers at Bobby Jones," recalled Bell. "We said, 'Is that right? Well, there's one on your course right now.'" Hill had registered and was on the course as they spoke. He was quickly corralled and, along with the others, escorted off the grounds.

It took two years of strategy sessions and late-night meetings between the golfers and a group of lawyer friends, but they eventually filed a lawsuit—Holmes vs. Atlanta—that sought to desegregate public golf courses and parks in the city. Roscoe E. Thomas was lead attorney but Tup was head instigator. "He was a mover and shaker," said Gary Holmes of his father. "And he was fearless." Not even numerous death threats caused him to back off. Dissatisfied with U.S. District Court Judge Boyd Sloan's 1954 ruling in the case that blacks had a Constitutional right to play golf but only in accordance with Atlanta's "separate but equal" precept, Holmes and his fellow litigants decided to appeal to a higher power. That's when John H. Calhoun, a businessman and president of the local chapter of the NAACP, got involved. He recommended the organization throw its clout behind the golfers; the NAACP responded by providing resources and the chief counsel of its legal defense team, an up-and-coming lawyer named Thurgood Marshall, to present their case before an appeals court in New Orleans. When that court upheld Judge Sloan's ruling, the golfers were forced to take their fight to the nation's ultimate battleground, the U.S. Supreme Court. This time they won. The Supreme Court accepted the case in the fall term of 1955 and, on Nov. 7, ruled in favor of the black golfers. "We were justifiably happy with the outcome," said Bell, in a classic bit of understatement.

Not everyone shared in their joy, especially Georgia Gov. Marvin Griffin who had added to an already incendiary climate by declaring, "Co-mingling of the races in Georgia state parks and recreation areas will not be tolerated." In an attempt to circumvent the ruling, Atlanta mayor William B. Hartsfield urged the city to sell its courses to individuals, who could then declare them open to private membership only. Although Hartsfield's effort failed, it fueled the growing anger of diehard Jim Crow preservationists. "We were definitely concerned about a reprisal," said Bell, who, along with the others, devised a plan to counter any potential uprising. On Dec. 24, 1955, Tup Holmes, Oliver Holmes and Charles Bell (Dr. Holmes decided to forego the formality) teed off at North Fulton Golf Course, avoiding even the possibility of a dark cloud at Bobby Jones GC obscuring their day in the sun. Atlanta's public courses were officially desegregated without incident.

"It's gratifying to know that I participated in something so meaningful," said Bell, the only survivor of the original foursome. Dr. Holmes died in September of 1965, Oliver nearly a year to the day later, and Tup succumbed to cancer in December of 1967. "He should have been dead in September but he refused until December," says Gary Holmes of his father's unwillingness to yield even to mortality. They are buried in a cemetery adjacent to Lincoln CC, which, ironically, had lost most of its patrons to city-owned courses by the mid-1970s and closed. In 1983, Atlanta Mayor Andrew Young renamed Adams Park Golf Course the Alfred F. (Tup) Holmes Memorial GC. Fittingly, it was maintained by the city for the enjoyment of all its citizenry, until 1986 when it was leased to the American Golf Management Company.

Georgia's disciples of desegregation inspired others to take their cases to court. In August 1954, U.S. District Judge T. M. Kennerly decreed that blacks had a right to play golf on municipal courses by virtue of a prior ordinance abolishing segregation on Houston's public courses. In November 1955, a suit was filed in federal court on behalf of African-Americans seeking access to golf facilities in Osceola, Fla. About the same time, four black golfers attempted to play a municipal course in Fort Lauderdale, Fla., but were turned away, supposedly because a tournament was in progress. Mayor P.G. Reynolds responded to their subsequent protest by declaring that there were no clubhouse facilities for

The New York Times

December 24, 1955

Atlanta to Open Links
Governor Deplores End of Golf Course Segregation

ATLANTA, Dec. 23 (AP)—Negroes will begin play on the city's public golf courses tomorrow with the approval of Mayor William B. Hartsfield, but with the disapproval of Gov. Martin Griffin.

The Mayor yielded to a United States District Court decree implementing an early Supreme Court decision against golf course segregation. He said that as an alternative the city could have sold its parks and closed the links, but this would have deprived 70,000 white players of the game and 100 city employees of their jobs just to deny "a few dozen Negro players" the use of the courses.

The Governor issued a statement deploring that the city "has chosen to throw in the towel" but saying there was nothing he could do about it. He said he had offered to help Atlanta with legislation to sell the courses as an alternative to integration but had been spurned.

black golfers at the course. He deemed desegregation of it uneconomical and entertained the idea of selling the facility to prevent play by African-Americans.

Reynolds' action was typical of many public officials in the wake of the Holmes vs. Atlanta case. The decision set off a mad scramble to avoid the inevitable. It also sparked various mayhem and creative chaos.

> Basically, what (*Judge Johnson J. Hayes*) said was that although the city (*Greensboro*) had leased the golf course, it still had an obligation to see to it that no one was discriminated against at the course.

George C. Simkins Jr. had closed his dental practice on East Market St. in Greensboro, N.C., almost every Wednesday since he first started beating golf balls at Nocho Park Golf Course in the late 1940s. Thus, it was not unusual for passersby to see Simkins standing in the parking lot of Arthur Lee's Shell service station across the street from his office with golf clubs in hand and a look of eager anticipation on his face. On the morning of December 7th 1955, an early winter day, Simkins awaited the arrival of five golf partners. The morning chill was nothing compared to the hot water in which they would find themselves before noon. "I'll never forget," recalled Dr. Simkins. "It was a beautiful day for golf."

Normally, Dr. Simkins and his friends would be among the first groups off the tee at Nocho Park, the 9-hole public layout in Greensboro frequented by black golfers. When they wanted a change of pace, they would meet at the Shell station and drive to High Point or Charlotte or Durham to play one of the few courses open to people of color. On this day, though, they planned to play Gillespie Park, a city-owned course operated as a private facility by a group of white citizens who leased it for $1. Lease agreements such as this were a common practice among Southern municipalities which sought to circumvent the Supreme Court ruling that made it unlawful for city-owned golf courses to discriminate against anyone. Play at Gillespie Park was restrict-

*The "Greensboro Six": (left to right) **Phillip Cook**, **Sam Murray**, **Elijah Herring**, **Joseph Sturdivant**, **George Simkins** and **Leon Wolfe** after their release from jail.*

ed to "members" and their guests. African-Americans fit neither category, but Dr. Simkins and his friends were determined to change that.

When they arrived at Gillespie Park, the golf shop attendant, a portly man of ruddy complexion, greeted them with the warmth of day-old grits. "He said we couldn't play, then grabbed the registration book to keep us from signing it," recalled Dr. Simkins. "We were determined, though."

One after another, Dr. Simkins, Leon Wolfe, Joseph Sturdivant, Samuel Murray, Elijah Herring and Phillip Cook defiantly placed their 75-cent green fee on the counter and headed for the first tee. They were on the fifth hole when head pro Ernie Edwards caught up with them. Brandishing a golf club, Edwards cursed at the sixsome, and threatened to have them arrested if they didn't leave. "He asked us why we were out

The New York Times

April 5, 1961

Sifford To Compete
North Carolina Club Accepts Negro Golfer for Open

GREENSBORO, N.C., April 4 (AP) — Charlie Sifford, who has won the national Negro golf championships five times, will compete in the Greater Greensboro open golf tournament April 13-16. He will be the first Negro to compete in a Southern tournament sponsored by the Professional Golfers Association.

Sifford, who plays with a cigar in his mouth, currently is among the top twenty-five money winners in golf. The board of directors of the Sedgefield Country Club, where the twenty-fourth annual $22,500 event will be held, approved Sifford's entry today.

Sifford shared the first-round lead in the San Francisco open this year and won $1,175. he was tied for third at Tucson, where he won $1,150. He captured the Almaden open in 1960, defeating Ken Venturi and Bob Rosburg, among others.

He won the national negro championships in 1953, 1954, 1955, 1956 and 1960. He is the only Negro ever to win a tournament on the P.G.A. circuit.

there," recalled Dr. Simkins. "I said, 'We're out here for a cause—the cause of democracy. We're taxpayers. This is a city golf course funded by our taxes and we should be allowed to play it.'" The golfers ignored Edwards' warning, finished nine holes and departed for home. Later that evening, a black police officer arrested the six dissidents and took them to the county jail. Dr. Simkins' father paid their bail and the fight to desegregate public golf courses in Greensboro ensued.

The six golfers were eventually found guilty of trespassing and sentenced to 30 days in jail. They lost an appeal in superior court, received an active jail sentence, but continued the fight at the federal court level. There, Judge Johnson J. Hayes ruled in their favor and issued a declaratory judgment. Basically, what he said was that although the city had leased the golf course, it still had an obligation to see to it that no one was discriminated against at the course. He ordered Gillespie Park opened to everyone within two weeks. However, that was not the end of the matter. Before the order could be enforced, someone slipped into the Gillespie Park clubhouse under cover of darkness and burned it to the ground. "Someone was determined to keep us from playing that course," Dr. Simkins said, "even if it meant they couldn't play it either." City officials refused to rebuild the clubhouse and closed the golf course. It was seven long years before nine holes were finally reopened to the public.

The "Greensboro Six" eventually appealed the original decision to the U.S. Supreme Court. They attempted to get Thurgood Marshall, chief counsel for the NAACP Legal Defense Fund, to represent them but he refused to take the case. "In Thurgood's opinion, we were wrong in the first place," Dr. Simkins said. "He felt we should have gotten an injunction to play the course. He said we would lose by one vote and that Justice Tom Clark would be the deciding vote. Sure enough, he was and we did." That Governor Luther Hodges commuted their sentences was small consolation. "I thought it was the right way

Asked if Shoal Creek members would feel comfortable bringing black guests to the club, (*Hall*) Thompson boiled his opinion down to one eight-word answer that would become one of the most notorious statements in the history of golf: "No, that's just not done in Birmingham, Alabama."

to go at the time," Dr. Simkins said, "but we went through so much hell, if I had it to do over I don't know if I'd go that way. I'd probably go the injunction route."

By the time Gillespie Park finally reopened in 1962—eight years after Brown vs. the Board of Education opened America's classrooms to people of all races—segregation on North Carolina's public golf courses had been eradicated. However, desegregating the country's private playgrounds would take more than personal sacrifice and doggedness. Someone had to unwittingly send up a flare to expose the discrimination practiced openly at private clubs, yet overlooked by the brokers of the game. Hall Thompson proved the unwitting man for the job; and Birmingham, Ala., where Dr. Martin Luther King officially launched the civil rights movement three decades earlier, proved the perfect stage.

The controversy arose when Thompson, owner of Thompson Tractor Co. and founder of Shoal Creek GC, was quoted in June 21, 1990, editions of the *Birmingham Post-Herald* saying the private club—slated to host the PGA Championship in less than two months—would not be pressured into accepting African-American mem-

The New York Times
June 22, 1990
P.G.A. Site Bars Blacks

BIRMINGHAM, Ala., June 21 (AP) — The Shoal Creek Country Club, which will be host to the P.G.A. Championship from Aug. 6 through Aug. 12, will not be forced into accepting blacks as members, its founder said today.

The founder, Hall Thompson, said the club's members included Jews, women, Lebanese and Italians but no blacks. "The country club is our home and we pick and choose who we want," he said, adding that members did not allow blacks because "that's just not done in Birmingham."

Thompson said blacks played at Shoal Creek during the 1984 P.G.A. Championship, and black caddies are allowed to play on Mondays, when the course is closed to members.

Officials with the Professional Golfers Association of America said if a club was found to be discriminating racially it could affect a decision to hold a future P.G.A. event there: But the 1990 tournament will go ahead as planned. The P.G.A.'s president, Pat Rielly, said in a telephone interview from Pasadena, Calif., that the organization had found no discriminatory written policies at Shoal Creek, but could do little if a club had unwritten rules.

Jim Awtrey, executive director of the P.G.A., said, "We don't condone discrimination," but that exclusionary practices were not a factor in choosing a site.

bers. Thompson said that black golfers had played the course during a tournament in 1984 and that it was open to its black caddies every Monday. "But we have the right to associate or not to associate with whomever we choose," he said. "The country club is our home and we pick and choose who we want." Asked if Shoal Creek members would feel comfortable bringing black guests to the club, Thompson boiled his opinion down to one eight-word answer that would become one of the most notorious statements in the history of golf: "No, that's just not done in Birmingham, Ala."

*Shoal Creek founder **Hall Thompson**, whose racially insensitive statements led to sweeping policy change among the game's ruling organizations.*

Reaction to Thompson's comments was immediate and full of indictment. The president of the city's chapter of the Southern Christian Leadership Conference (SCLC) called for Shoal Creek to integrate immediately or else. The NAACP threatened to picket the PGA Championship. Corporate sponsors of the championship, afraid of getting caught in the public relations fallout, began to pull their advertising from the ABC telecast, costing the network an estimated $2 million in revenue. The flap seemed to take on a life of its own. Not even an attempted mediation by Birmingham's black third-term mayor, Richard Arrington, or a contrite apology from Thompson could calm the waters. Stuck right in the middle, somewhere between purgatory and eternal damnation, were golf's governing bodies in this country—the PGA of America, USGA and PGA Tour. What surfaced as the key issue, far overshadowing the longstanding exclusionary practices of private country clubs, was the integrity of the selection process these organizations used to pick their championship sites. Could golf's governing bodies withstand the political, moral and financial ramifi-

Louis J. Willie, a Birmingham insurance executive, was named an honorary member of Shoal Creek in order to quell the furor over Hall Thompson's unfortunate remarks.

Grant Spaeth was president of the USGA during the Shoal Creek incident.

cations from choosing sites that practiced discrimination, written or otherwise? It didn't take long for those caught in the crossfire to weigh in.

"We don't condone discrimination," said Jim Awtrey, chief executive officer of the PGA of America.

Said USGA President C. Grant Spaeth, "Since the Birmingham question, there have been several clubs in line to host future championships considering withdrawing the bid because of the current climate. We can't tell them what to do, nor advise them. It appears a private club's practices will no longer be private when they ask to host an event."

The PGA Tour issued a statement saying a proposal would be presented to its Tournament Policy Board that, if approved, would alter the selection process for host sites. The statement intimated that a club's exclusionary practices would be called into question.

Through his role as peacemaker, Mayor Arrington could be credited with saving the PGA Championship from a permanent black eye. He worked diligently with the PGA of America, Shoal Creek and Birmingham's black leaders to reach a compromise that included immediate membership at the club for a prominent black businessman. Two weeks before the championship, 66-year-old Louis Willie, president of the Booker T. Washington Insurance Co., was made an honorary member at Shoal Creek. "I did not volunteer for this," said Willie, "but the mayor sent word he would like for me to do this. I am doing it for the community."

Shoal Creek, site of the 1990 PGA Championship.

African-American golfers were vocal in their criticism of the compromise. Said Charlie Owens, "You need a tub of water and you get a teardrop and you're satisfied? No, it didn't go far enough." Lee Elder agreed. "Either these clubs are going to have to be integrated or we do not play them," he said. "It's going to be as simple as that."

Golf's governing bodies heard the rumblings and took steps to avoid another Shoal Creek incident. At its board of directors meeting on August 7, the PGA of America adopted a policy that eliminated golf clubs with discriminatory practices from being considered as sites for the PGA Championship. Said PGA president Patrick J. Rielly, "The PGA recognizes that private clubs have a legal right to determine their own membership policies, but as a leader in golf, the PGA also recognizes

*At the end of one of the most tumultuous championships in the game's history, **Wayne Grady** won the PGA at Shoal Creek.*

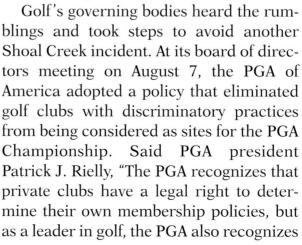

its obligations to foster and promote equal opportunity in the game." Other residents of golf's head table recognized their obligation, too. The PGA Tour followed the PGA's lead, its policy board approving new guidelines that prohibited the tour from staging events at "any golf club that has membership policies that discriminate on the basis of race, religion, sex or national origin." Said then-tour commissioner Deane Beman, "We don't want to lose any of our tournament sites, but if it happens, so be it." Only Butler National GC in Oak Brook, Ill., which had hosted the Western Open since 1974, and Cypress Point Club in Pebble Beach, Calif., part of the three-course rotation of the AT&T Pebble Beach National Pro-Am since 1947, refused to comply. They were dropped as tournament sites in 1991.

Ron Townsend, the first African-American member of Augusta National Golf Club.

The USGA, golf's oldest and most powerful ruling body, reshaped its championship site guidelines in November 1990. Two months prior to that, however, a group of green-jacketed white men huddled in conference in Augusta, Ga. Out of the meeting came an announcement that illustrated more than anything else Shoal Creek's impact on America's collective conscience. Ron Townsend, a 49-year-old television executive from Jacksonville, Fla., had accepted an invitation to become Augusta National Golf Club's first African-American member. Present at the Masters every April since, Townsend has been a highly visible symbol of the struggle for equal access and acceptance waged by some persistent predecessors. He is also victory personified.

CHAPTER 8

TEDDY, CHARLIE AND LEE: THE INVISIBLE MEN

"But if it hadn't been for the good Lord, a lot of days I would have taken one of those golf clubs and started swinging."
—*Charlie Sifford, on keeping a cool head and a promise to Jackie Robinson.*

L eaning back in a golf cart, the elderly gentleman adjusted his dark glasses and clamped down hard on the cigar jutting from his jaw. "I can't even get into Super Senior tournaments," he said, his voice trembling. "At least I could get my expenses out of the Super Seniors."

The few fans and tournament workers who passed him on this sweltering summer day in San Antonio in 1996 wouldn't have noticed, but Charlie Sifford, the man who broke golf's color barrier, was a broken man himself. Pieces of his jigsaw-puzzle life lay scattered across the country at the end of a journey that defined an American hero. It was nearly 35 years ago at this PGA Tour stop, the Texas Open, that several pistol-packing security guards warned Sifford that he would be entering the grounds at his own risk. All he wanted was to play golf but those in authority wouldn't let him. Charlie's dignity turned and walked away, but his battered pride, which had been chipped and scarred since he took up the game as a youth, suffered another bruise.

Now, Sifford had returned to the Texas Open as a guest of the tournament committee. He was there to schmooze and be schmoozed, and to watch Tiger Woods, whom he considered a surrogate grandson, try to win a second straight tour event in his rookie season. Sifford's own golf career had been chugging towards the end for several years. Except for the occasional corporate outing and sponsor's exemption into a Senior PGA Tour event, opportunities to play were few and far between for a player of his age and position on the money list. "It really makes me feel bad, especially since I've supported these tournaments for all these years," Sifford said of his inability to get into senior tournament fields. The twilight of his career was proving to be no different from its dawning. Golf either shunned him or ignored him; it never embraced him. Sifford, who deserved better if only for his endurance in the face of tremendous adversity, was golf's invisible man. He had no more status in the game than his friend and contemporary, Teddy Rhodes, arguably the most talented golfer of color before Woods. He might have had even less than Lee Elder, who followed through the door that Sifford helped open, and went on to achieve greater success on both the regular and senior tours. Individually, the three African-Americans are icons in the eyes of those who acknowledge their roles in the evolution of professional golf, even if the game has often looked the other way.

Charlie Sifford and his ever-present cigar. Sifford, introduced to golf as a caddie in North Carolina, grew up to become one of the most outspoken figures in the game's history.

In his autobiography *Just Let Me Play*, Sifford described Rhodes as incomparable, but, unfortunately, ahead of his time. Wrote Sifford, "Poor Teddy just came along 20 years too soon to be a black man in professional golf. Although he tried a couple of times to break into the PGA Tour, he was just too nice a guy and too much a gentleman to fight and scratch for his constitutional right to play. Teddy didn't want any of that pushing and pressing that it took to break into the game. It was contrary to his nature."

> "Poor Teddy just came along 20 years too soon to be a black man in professional golf. Although he tried a couple of times to break into the PGA Tour, he was just too nice a guy and too much a gentleman to fight and scratch for his constitutional right to play."
>
> — Charlie Sifford

That non-confrontational temperament was shaped on the playgrounds and in the caddie yards of Nashville, Tenn., where Theodore Rhodes was reared in a small, God-fearing home on the north side of town. When the other caddies at Belle Meade and Richland country clubs teased him about his tattered clothes, young Teddy rarely got ruffled. He brushed off verbal assaults even then and wore the nickname "Rags" from preadolescence in the early 1920s to preeminence on the black golf tour in the 1950s. Burned deep into his essence was an ex-caddie's desire to play golf and compete at the highest level. "He was a dreamer," said his daughter, Peggy White. "He lived to play golf. It was his passion."

Rhodes' love for the game grew despite his being denied access to the public courses in Nashville. While most of his peers were being taught the merits of a good education, Teddy was perfecting caddie shots on red-clay fields. He was undefeated on his field of dreams against stalwarts on the PGA Tour such as Johnny Farrell and Walter Hagen, whose stylish dress Rhodes would one day emulate, giving his nickname a totally different meaning. However, Rhodes never went from rags to riches. His only means of escaping the hand-to-mouth existence prevalent in the South was to enlist in the Navy during World War II. When he returned to Nashville after the war, he found the same policies of segregation awaiting him. Ultimately, his game blossomed on the military courses near Nashville.

Rhodes' career began and ended in the relative obscurity of tournaments conducted by and for people of color. However, on rare occasions, black players were welcomed into events with primarily Caucasian fields. In fact, it was an invitation to play in Chicago at the 1946 Tam O'Shanter, one of the few white-run tour-

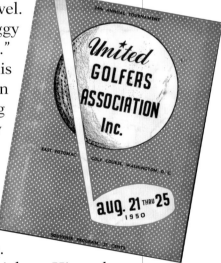

Program for the 1950 UGA Championship, won by Teddy Rhodes.

naments opened to African-Americans, that unlocked a small window of opportunity for the man Sifford called "the black Jack Nicklaus." Played over the Fourth of July weekend, the Tam O'Shanter was not sponsored by the PGA Tour but many of its regulars played in the event. Rhodes' presence drew stares from the mostly white galleries. At 5 feet 11 inches and of medium build, with dashing good looks, a processed hairstyle and natty attire, he struck quite a figure. He was also the only black player in the field that year and clearly felt uncomfortable with the attention. The chilly reception he received from some of the white players disconcerted him. Although he was 32, the Tam O'Shanter was his first

Bill Spiller (left) with three-time Masters winner *Jimmy Demaret* (middle) and *Teddy Rhodes* (right).

exposure to huge, hostile crowds. But, true to his natural demeanor, Rhodes quietly competed and managed a respectable 43rd place finish, worth $150. Said two-time PGA champion Paul Runyan, "He had great skill and technique. If he had had the same advantages that we white kids had, I think he might have been a real contender. But during those days, the black kids were playing under a cloud. They were not as welcome as they should have been and as a result they didn't get a fair shot."

Rhodes excelled where he was welcome—on the UGA. Later that year, he finished runner-up to Howard Wheeler for the 1946 Negro National Open title in Pittsburgh, his first taste of success on the national level. He would go on to win the UGA championship in 1949, '50, '51 and '57.

In those days, UGA tournaments were social events in the local African-American community, frequented by celebrities du jour and superstar athletes in other arenas. It was at one of those tournaments—the Joe Louis Invitational at Rackham GC in Detroit—that Rhodes was to meet his golfing savior. Louis, a golf junkie, recognized Rhodes' potential and hired him as his "personal golf instructor," a euphemism, since what Louis became, in effect, was Rhodes' sponsor, benefactor and friend. That winter Louis sent Rhodes to Los Angeles to develop his game under the tutelage of Ray Mangrum, brother of 1946 U.S. Open winner Lloyd Mangrum. The municipal courses of Los Angeles County became Rhodes' home and venues of opportunity. His pinpoint short-iron game and

Teddy Rhodes as he appeared on a magazine cover.

scrambling ability often minimized gambling losses incurred through his partnership with Louis, whose common sense appeared overmatched by his ego when it came to betting on golf. "Hell, he couldn't play that well," said Sifford. "He could shoot about a 75 or 77 or something like that. He might get it around par

Joe Louis playing in a UGA event.

if he was really on. But to beat Joe Louis wasn't no big deal." It was, however, very profitable for some hustlers, including Smiley Quick, who won the 1946 U.S. Amateur Public Links and finished runner-up in the U.S. Amateur the same year. Legend has it that Quick bought two apartment buildings with his winnings off Louis. But the boxing champ never minded losing to Rhodes. In his book, *Joe Louis—50 Years an American Hero*, Louis' son, Joe Louis Barrow Jr., recalled one incident when Rhodes was having a hard time paying his bills: "Rhodes asked Leonard Reed, the champ's personal secretary, to ask Louis to lend him $200 to pay his rent. Knowing that Rhodes needed another $200 for food—and that the promising young golfer could beat him handily—Louis suggested they play a round for $400. He lost and happily paid Rhodes the money. The fledgling golfer, while keeping his dignity, paid his rent."

Joe Louis in his boxing days.

While on Louis' payroll, Rhodes developed into a player who could hold his own—when given the opportunity. One of those opportunities came during the 1948 U.S. Open at Riviera CC in Los Angeles, practically in Rhodes' backyard. In fact, Rhodes was familiar with the course, having finished 21st in a field of 66 at the Los Angeles Open held there in January. It was after that non-sanctioned PGA tournament that he, Bill Spiller and amateur Madison Gunther sued the PGA of America for not allowing them to play at the tour's next stop, in Richmond, Calif. The issue wouldn't be resolved until September when the PGA agreed to stop closing its events to African-Americans and the trio dropped the suit. In June, however, Rhodes wasn't so much concerned about pending litigation as he was golf's national championship. Taking advantage of local knowledge and accuracy off the tee, Rhodes opened with a one-under-par 70 to trail Ben Hogan and defending champion Lew Worsham by three shots. The aftershocks from his first round were felt in caddie yards around the country and in juke joints from South Central L.A. to Harlem, N.Y. Said Charles E. (Eddie) Miller, who presided over qualifying for USGA events for four decades, "I remember it as if it was yesterday. He (Rhodes) was quite a player, quite a swinger of the golf club. He had a huge gallery. And he scared the hell out of some Southerners after that round," a reference to the fact that the top 24 finishers in the U.S. Open received invitations to the Masters. The Rhodes "scare" was short-lived. He shot 76-77-79 the rest of the way to finish at 302, tied for 51st, 26 shots behind Hogan, who won the first of his four U.S. Opens.

Joe Louis, the retired heavyweight champion, tries out a new putter just acquired by his protegé, ***Bill Spiller***, who was admitted to the Phoenix Open Golf Tournament after a change in the PGA of America's "Caucasian-only" Rule.

Rhodes returned to the less lucrative but friendlier confines of the UGA for the remainder of the season. In August, he posted a 72-hole total of three-over-par 291 at Engineers GC on Long Island to win the inaugural Ray Robinson Open. He won $4,256 in official money that year. (In contrast, Hogan, the Player of the Year on the PGA Tour, won $32,112.) Rhodes conquered his nerves in the twin Tam O'Shanter events in 1949 and had his most impressive performance outside the UGA. First, he tied for 35th in the All-American; then, the following week, he tied for 14th in the World Championship of Golf, thanks in large part to a third-round 69. Said Tam O'Shanter promoter George S. May, "Teddy is a great golfer. All he needs is an opportunity to play in more big-time tournaments." Those opportunities were difficult to come by, but Rhodes rarely complained. Instead, he made the best of those that did come his way.

Eventually, Rhodes met and befriended a young newcomer to the UGA named Charlie Sifford. Rhodes' easygoing style was a salve to Sifford's wounds. He was both conscience and confidant to his junior adversary, sharing laughs and tears on life's long road trip. "Joe [Louis] bought Teddy this little old red Buick in '49," recalled Sifford, "and Teddy couldn't drive. We went to Cleveland to play in the Negro National Open and I went over to Detroit to pick up Ted's car. He named the car 'Alexander.' We put about 200,000 miles on that car. The floorboard broke in on us. Well, we'd be going down the highway and ol' Teddy would fall asleep. I'd be doing about 65 or 70. Teddy would wake up and say, 'Hey, Hoss, man don't run Alexander that hard.'"

In 1950, Rhodes slowed down himself a little that year with his marriage to Claudia Oliver and the birth of his daughter, Deborah. (He was already a dedicated father to his daughter, Peggy, born from an earlier relationship with Ollie Crenshaw of

Nashville.) In 1952, two years before leaving the employ of Louis, he joined Sifford, Spiller and the champ as the first group of blacks to compete in a PGA of America-sponsored tournament, the Phoenix Open. He eventually played in 69 PGA events in his career (his season high was 11 in 1956), earning a check 24 times, nine of them for top-20 finishes.

Rhodes remained a contender on the UGA into the late 1950s, despite failing health due to a kidney ailment that sapped his strength and made playing in four-day tournaments difficult. He beat Sifford by three strokes for the Negro National Open title in '57 and collected two more crowns (the Gotham Open and Progressive GC championship in Peoria, Ill.) the next year. In 1960, he was part of an African-American contingent invited to

1961 UGA annual meeting in Cincinnati.

play in Havana by the Cuban government. By the time the PGA rescinded its Caucasian-only clause in November of 1961, Rhodes had retired from competitive golf. He settled into the life of a respected golf instructor, first in St. Louis, then in Chicago. He taught Lee Elder the nuances of wedge play by having the young Texan hit hundreds of shots between fairways at Forest Park, a public track in St. Louis. When Althea Gibson made the transition from tennis to golf in the early 1960s, she went to Rhodes for help with her short game. He spent many hours softening her hands and disposition at Cumberland Golf Course in Nashville. While teaching satisfied his

Shirley Temple with Teddy Rhodes and friend.

need to share, nothing stirred his soul like the thrill of competition. After retirement, he lived vicariously through the careers of Sifford, Pete Brown, Rafe Botts, Elder and others. His spirit accompanied them in locker rooms where they were not welcome. His deteriorating health both saddened and inspired them.

Rhodes died on July 4, 1969, in Nashville. His immortality in a game for which he was seemingly born never materialized. There are monuments to his career, which included more than 150 victories, according to daughter Peggy's count. Two years after his death, Nashville officials renamed the nine-hole Cumberland Golf Course after him. In 1993, the city christened an 18-hole daily-fee layout in his honor. Five years later, he was inducted into the Tennessee Hall of Fame. Posthumous honors aside, the golf world will forever wonder just how great Rhodes would have been had he been given an equal

> As a tribute to Rhodes' unwavering spirit, Nashville golf enthusiasts formed the Ted Rhodes Foundation in 1970, with a goal of assisting young golfers in establishing and maintaining careers in golf.

chance. Wrote Sifford, "By the time things opened up a little bit for me in the early sixties, Teddy was too old and too sick to play...He was a fine man, a good friend and a great golfer."

As a tribute to Rhodes' unwavering spirit, Nashville golf enthusiasts formed the Ted Rhodes Foundation in 1970, with a goal of assisting young golfers in establishing and maintaining careers in golf. Peggy White assumed control of the organization and renamed it the Ted Rhodes Foundation, Inc. Its main fundraising effort is a tournament held annually in August. Fittingly, it is a throwback to the old UGA events where Rhodes' image continues to rule. Said White, "The foundation insures all the high goals of my father will continue to be realized."

It took Sifford six years to beat Rhodes, but it has taken him much longer to reconcile the roadblocks he, like his mentor, had to overcome. His candor and honesty have branded him a bitter old man. In some circles, he is to golf what Jackie Robinson was to baseball. In others, he is a pariah who should have been muzzled years ago. Wrote Sifford in *Just Let Me Play*, "There is no place for

*Teddy Rhodes chats on the practice green with pro **Ralph Guldahl** (left) and **Justin Grant**, a noted golf hustler.*

a black man in professional golf. It doesn't take a Philadelphia lawyer to figure that one out. I'm 69 years old, and I've been playing this game since I was a little kid in North Carolina. I played for 15 years on the PGA circuit, and I've been a regular on the Senior PGA Tour since its inception in 1980. And I still don't see any room for a black in golf."

Sifford's cynical view of the game was shaped by myriad negative experiences. As a caddie at Carolina Country Club in Charlotte, N.C., the development of his game was temporarily stymied by club members, who didn't want a young black man playing their course. There was the degrading incident at the 1952 Phoenix Open, when he and his all-black foursome reached the first green only to find the cup filled with human excrement. His first trip back home to North Carolina as an approved PGA professional in 1961 was marred by the sentiments of the Old South—racial slurs, hate mail and death threats. The pain from Masters snubs, real or imagined, still burns within his chest. "I can't even talk about it," he says. "It makes my blood boil just to think about it." If Sifford sounds bitter, perhaps it is justified.

> At the Long Beach Open ... Sifford became the first African-American to win an open tournament against a field that included many of the country's best golfers ...

Sifford lists the four most influential people in his life as his wife, Rose, Teddy Rhodes, Billy Eckstine and Jackie Robinson. He might have added two more—Carolina CC owner and head pro Sutton Alexander and PGA pro Clayton Heafner. The latter took Sifford under his wing in 1938 and taught the then-16-year-old caddie how to handle winning and losing with equanimity. An accomplished member of the PGA Tour, Heafner frequented Carolina CC and often had Sifford on his bag. Other times the two competed head-to-head on Mondays when caddies were allowed to play the course. Sifford analyzed Heafner's game and incorporated parts of it into his. But, as his reputation grew at the club, so did the resentment among some members who objected to his being able to play the course. Sensing an insurrection that might prove dangerous to young Charlie, Alexander convinced Sifford's parents to send him north where the atmosphere was more tolerant. In the winter of 1939, Charlie was dispatched to Philadelphia to live with his uncle, James Sifford. That's where he found Cobbs Creek, a city-owned course where blacks and whites played alongside each other without incident. There, the second stage of Sifford's golf career began in earnest.

Charlie Sifford.

Sifford learned a quick lesson in humility during his first match at Cobbs Creek. Local legend Howard Wheeler, who played cross-handed and demonstrated his prowess by executing all sorts of trick shots, taught the impetuous young golfer about the tenuous relationship between a fool and his money. "I was working at National Biscuit Company," recalled Sifford. "I didn't even have my own clubs then, so I borrowed a set from a friend. I saw Howard playing cross-handed and said, 'I believe I can beat him.' Howard took my $10 before I knew what had happened. Man, he could play. He was one of the greatest black players of all time." Indeed, Wheeler, a transplant from Georgia, won the Negro National Open five times, but never gave the PGA Tour a second thought. "He was content being the local favorite," said Sifford, who had bigger plans for his career. Upon returning from a stint in the U.S. Army, Sifford married Rose Crumbley, a pretty, petite, young lady he'd met at a dance several years earlier and fallen for immediately. He then set out to make a living playing golf.

Clayton Heafner, who hired a young Charlie Sifford to be his caddie, and later nurtured his playing career.

His first big break came at the 1946 Negro National Open in Pittsburgh where he met the famous singer and bandleader, Billy Eckstine. At Rhodes' suggestion, Eckstine hired Sifford as his personal golf pro and valet, setting up an arrangement similar to the one between Rhodes and Joe Louis. Sifford prospered in the relationship for the better part of 10 years, touring with Eckstine during the winter months and playing the UGA in the summer. He finally dethroned Rhodes as UGA national champion in 1952 and reeled off an unprecedented five consecutive national titles before Rhodes returned the favor in 1957. Sifford would reclaim the crown in 1960, but the warm and fuzzy feeling he got from dominating the black golf tour hardly quenched his thirst for the big time. "I didn't want to beat black people at golf," he said. "I wanted to beat the white people at golf." Sifford faced the same stumbling block as every other person of color who sought to enter PGA of America events—the Caucasian-only clause. He performed well in the few tournaments with mixed fields for which he and other black players were eligible. At the 1955 Canadian Open, he shot a career-best 63 to take the first-round lead. Arnold Palmer eventually won the tournament by four strokes over Jack Burke Jr., but for one day Sifford was the best golfer in the world. Two years later at the Long Beach Open, a PGA co-sponsored event (but not considered an "official" event because it was only 54 holes), he was the best for an entire week. Using a putter given him by Joe Louis, Sifford shot a final-round 64 to tie Eric Monti, then defeated Monti on the third playoff hole. Sifford thus became the first African-American to win an open tournament against a field that included many of the country's best golfers, including Gene Littler, Paul Harney, Jerry Barber, Gay Brewer, Ed Oliver, Jack Fleck, Jim Turnesa and Tommy Bolt.

"This is the greatest thing that has ever happened," said Sifford, then 34, displaying the exuberance of a rookie. "This is what I've been waiting for. I hope I'll be really able to go." By then, Sifford had a wife and child to support. He also had the extra burden of an entire race on his shoulders. Recalled Sifford years later, "Man, it's tough to win when you've got to win, when you need that dough and when you've got every Negro on your back, pulling for you."

The pressure only got worse, especially after Sifford's perseverance placed him at the head of the pack in the push for equal opportunity. Jackie Robinson wrote a column in *The New York Post* in 1959 blasting PGA officials for continuing to discriminate against Sifford and other black players. That same year California attorney general Stanley Mosk started applying a vise grip on the PGA in an attempt to squeeze the Caucasian-only clause from its constitution. By the end of the year, the PGA had cleared the way for Sifford to become an approved tournament player. He received a "tour card" in March of 1960, making him the first African-American eligible to play the tour schedule. But it would take another year for the Caucasian-only clause to be stripped from the PGA's constitution and another four for Sifford to gain full PGA membership. Sifford claimed the original tour card gave him only limited access to tour events. "It didn't mean anything," he said. "It didn't get me past those big ol' guards with those big ol' 45s."

> To his credit, Sifford never quit pushing. In August of 1967, that determination finally paid off in a full-fledged PGA Tour victory.

Like it or not, Sifford would be the gate crasher and a prime target for harassment. Jackie Robinson, who'd faced many of the same experiences when he broke baseball's color line in 1947, had recognized Sifford's potential as a lightning rod when the two met years earlier. "He asked me if I was a quitter," recalled Sifford. "I told him no. He said, 'If you're not a quitter you're probably going to experience some things that will make you want to quit. You can go out there and take one of those golf clubs and slap someone up side their head, but you better take it and go on about your business.' I promised him I would. But if it hadn't been for the good Lord, a lot of days I would have taken one of those golf clubs and started swinging."

Sifford's patience couldn't have been more taxed than during his homecoming as a PGA pro. Dr. George Simkins Jr., a Greensboro (N.C.) dentist and activist, convinced officials of the Greater Greensboro Open to invite Sifford to play in their tournament in 1961. Dr. Simkins had known Sifford from the latter's UGA days, when he won Dr. Simkins' tournament, the Gate City Open, in 1953 and '54. Simkins arranged for Sifford to stay in a dormitory at North Carolina A&T University because of the scarcity of hotels in the city that accepted African-Americans. But the students' late-night partying prevented Sifford from getting much sleep, so after two nights he moved out of the dorm and into the house of George Lavett. The first night there, he received

Jackie Robinson teaching his son, Jackie Jr., to play golf.

a telephone death threat. As he walked the fairways of Sedgefield CC the next day, racial slurs rained down on him from the mostly white galleries. Somehow Sifford endured the Old South hostility and finished fourth in the tournament, an amazing accomplishment. Wrote Sifford, "I hadn't won the tournament in Greensboro, but I felt a larger victory. I had come through my first southern tournament with the worst kind of social pressures and discrimination around me, and I hadn't cracked. I hadn't quit."

Charlie Sifford won his first PGA Tour event at the Greater Hartford Open in 1967 but it didn't gain him the one thing he wanted most — an invitation to the Masters.

To his credit, Sifford never quit pushing. In August of 1967, that determination finally paid off in a full-fledged PGA Tour victory. Thanks to another sizzling closing round, a 64, he won the Greater Hartford Open at Wethersfield CC, edging Steve Oppermann by one stroke. When the representative of the corporate sponsor handed him the $20,000 winner's check, Sifford could barely hold back the tears. "If you try hard enough," he said, "anything can happen."

Almost anything, that is. He would win again at the Los Angeles Open two years later. He would amass more than $340,000 in PGA Tour earnings, and another $1 million on the Senior PGA Tour. But he never earned the one thing in golf that was most important to him—an invitation to play in the Masters. The disappointment of not earning an invitation was such a bone of contention with Sifford that he regularly leveled charges of discrimination at Masters officials and openly challenged their selection process. Sifford's constant criticism sparked several reactions from Augusta National, one of which made newspaper headlines in November of 1968. It read: "Each year there are numbers of disappointed golfers who fail to qualify for a Masters Tournament invitation. Sometimes one or more express their unhappiness and their remarks find their way into print. We understand their feelings and normally make no response. In Mr. Sifford's case, we shall make an exception because he has several times publicized his displeasure about not receiving a player invitation and now intimates that his color is a factor. Every USA golfer, regardless of his racial background, has an opportunity to qualify for a Masters Tournament invitation and we doubt that anyone seriously expects us to change these Qualification Regulations in order to accommodate one particular person. Sifford is well aware of the various opportunities open to him to qualify and he also knows that if he is successful, an invitation will be forthcoming. Despite the remarks ascribed to him, we wish him well." It was signed, "Masters Tournament Committee."

A year later, Robert T. Jones Jr., responded to allegations Sifford made in a column written by Jim Murray of the *Los Angeles Times*. In the letter to Murray, Jones refuted Sifford's claim that Jones had threatened him. In closing he wrote, "It seems completely obvious to me that we cannot invite any golfer simply because he is black. This year, however, Sifford has made a very good start by winning the Los Angeles Open. It is, therefore, entirely likely that he could qualify under our regulation 14. This, however, will be entirely up to him." According to regulation 14, the six professionals on the PGA circuit not otherwise eligible who establish the best full year showing from the finish of the last Masters Tournament to the start of the next Masters Tournament received an invitation. Had Sifford been among the top six players on the PGA Tour, based on earnings or some other points system, over

Sifford today: though he rarely competes anymore, he is a close friend of Tiger Woods.

the 12-month period leading up to the 1969 Masters, he would have qualified. Going into the Greater Greensboro Open, the event prior to the Masters, Sifford was among the players in contention for the invitations. Others included Ron Cerrudo, Jack Montgomery, Bob Dickson, Bob Lunn, Dale Douglass, Ken Still, Mac McLendon, R.H. Sikes and Deane Beman. After the GGO, Lunn, Douglass, Still, McLendon, Sikes and Beman earned the coveted invitations. Sifford never came that close again. In 1971, Masters officials changed the qualifying regulations to players who win a tour event from one Masters to the next, making it retroactive from the '71 Masters to the event in '72. Sifford's tour victory in Los Angeles was his last. He wears on his heart the scars from never having met Masters qualifications. During Tiger Woods' historic Masters victory in 1997, Sifford's presence was felt through telegrams of encouragement he sent the young phenom. But he has never set foot on Augusta National's hallowed grounds.

While Sifford watched Woods blitz the field at Augusta National from his living room in Kingwood, Texas, Lee Elder witnessed it as a member of Woods' gallery. He walked in the shadows of the gigantic Georgia pines silently cheering a man of color's accomplishment just as his friends and supporters had done 22 years earlier, when he became the first African-American to be invited to play in the Masters. That he successfully completed the journey from nowhere to everywhere was a testimony to his tenacity and a tribute to Rhodes, Sifford and all the others who preceded him.

Robert Lee Elder was born July 14, 1934, in Dallas. One of eight siblings, he discovered the hard side of life when both his parents died before he reached maturity. Older sister Sadie Williams took charge of their tiny house on Phillip Street and finished raising the family. Lee, who eventually went to live with his aunt, Helen Harris, in Wichita Falls, Texas, was lured to the golf course

During Tiger Woods' historic Masters victory in 1997, Sifford's presence was felt through telegrams of encouragement he sent the young phenom. But he has never set foot on Augusta National's hallowed grounds.

out of necessity. He didn't need sixth-grade math to confirm what he already knew: any additional income he brought into the home could mean the difference between one meal or three. He reported to the all-white Tennison Park Golf Club intent on improving his lot in life and found not only an escape from his current circumstances but the key to his future. Lee and several other caddies were favored by Tennison head pro Erwin Hardwick, who looked the other way when they slipped onto the course late in the afternoon and played the six holes that were obscured from view of the clubhouse. After their loops, Elder and close friend Moses Brooks would often make a beeline for the Goodwill Store on Elm St. to spend any extra cash they had on golf equipment. They could get wooden-shafted clubs for 50 cents apiece and all the balls they could scavenge for free. As they developed as players, Elder and his friends teamed in some low-dollar matches at Oak Cliff, a prairie-flat course in east Dallas with more tumbleweeds than grass. By his early teens, Elder had developed into a player good enough to warrant financial backing. He received it from a character full of chutzpah and slicks named Alvin C. Thomas, but better known by his nom de golf—Titanic Thompson. Thompson was a world-class hustler, con artist, and, to Elder and Brooks, trusted friend.

Lee Elder, the first African-American to compete in the Masters.

"Titanic Thompson would come to town and stay most of the summer," said Brooks. "Lee and I would caddie for him, and he'd set up matches for us with different city players. He was the best I ever saw at baiting a player. He'd do stuff like dress us up in chauffeur's clothes and bet that he could take his chauffeur as a partner and beat a club's best players. He would rent property near a golf course and put a guy on a tractor in view of his group when they reached a certain hole. To con them into raising the bet, he'd say, 'I'll take that guy sitting on that tractor and play you for anything you want.' He taught me a valuable lesson one time when he had set up a match with some black caddies. I didn't want to play against them, so he went and got $1,000 worth of bills in different denominations. He gave me $500 and kept $500. He told me to throw mine in the hat and then he threw his in. Then he told me to reach in there and pick out the black money. His point was that all money is green, so go play and get it. I never forgot that." Neither did Elder. He and Thompson were hustling partners well into Elder's 20s. Even as a teenager, though, Elder honed in on serious competition, which was admittedly limited for African-Americans in those days. He found it once a year in a statewide amateur championship held exclusively for black players. He would win it in 1952, a year after a brush with fame that was both intimidating and inspirational.

> "Lee didn't think any man could beat him."
>
> — Moses Brooks

In the summer of 1951, Elder and Brooks loaded into a friend's car and headed for Cleveland and the Negro National Open at Seneca GC. Brooks faced boxing great Joe Louis in the semifinals of the championship flight for amateurs. Elder and his opponent made up the rest of the foursome. "I was so nervous that I just gave him the first four holes," recalled Brooks. "Then Joe did something totally unexpected. He looked me in the eye and said, 'I'm just a man like any other man. Don't be making me out to be no god.' That calmed me down a little bit and I played better the rest of the match, but I still lost, 2 and 1." Elder won his match and, having seen Louis' game, was confident he could beat the champ. "Lee didn't think any man could beat him," said Brooks. "When he was playing his best, no man could." Louis did, 2 and 1, but Elder made him work for the win.

Alvin C. Thomas, A.K.A. "Titanic Thompson," Lee Elder's one-time barnstorming partner.

Elder officially turned pro in 1959 and, thanks to a substantial stake from Los Angeles night club owner Moses Stevens, set out to dominate the black golf tours. He won four UGA Negro National Opens from 1963-1967. During one phenomenal stretch in 1966, he won 18 of the 22 tournaments he entered. "My friend, Jimmy McMillan, and I would drive my new Buick Deuce-and-a-Quarter all down through Macon (Ga.), Atlanta and Miami, and through Robbinsville, Ill., Chicago, Detroit," Elder said. "Wherever they had a tournament, that's where we'd go." The barnstorming enabled Elder to stockpile enough savings to try the PGA Tour's qualifying school in November of 1967. After documenting savings of $6,500—a requirement for prospective PGA Tour members in those days—Elder left his home in Washington, D.C., for West Palm Beach, Fla. He easily qualified, joining a rookie class that included Deane Beman, Ron Cerrudo, Marty

Fleckman, Bob Murphy and Tony Jacklin. In December, he launched his tour career by teaming with Pete Brown in the Haig & Haig Four-Ball at Los Coyotes CC in Buena Park, Calif. Black tourists often played together, stayed together and prayed together, exhibiting a solidarity in the mid-'60s and early '70s that served as a shield against diehard racist attitudes. In his first year on tour, Elder encountered at almost every stop the same treatment that had already hardened Sifford, Brown, Rafe Botts and others. At Pensacola (Fla.) CC, site of the Monsanto Open, Elder and the other black players weren't allowed to enter the clubhouse. The parking lot was their dressing room and dining facility. They had to use the bathroom in the caddie quarters. "I said I'd never go back to Pensacola after the way we were treated," Elder said.

Unlike Sifford, Elder chose a more apolitical route. The closest he came to bucking authority came when he was a teenager and he and two friends sneaked into the gallery at the Colonial National Invitational tournament in Fort Worth. When security discovered Elder and his buddies had no tickets, they were unceremoniously escorted from the premises. "That's all right," Elder told his friends. "One day I'll be walking down that fairway and they won't be able to put me out." He eventually returned to Fort Worth as a player instead of spectator. His arrival on the tour was trumpeted by a showdown with arguably the greatest golfer of all time.

The face-off occurred during Elder's rookie season at the American Golf Classic in Akron, Ohio. Elder finished regulation play tied with Jack Nicklaus and Frank Beard. Though he didn't win the playoff (Nicklaus did), Elder won something more important—the respect of golf fans around the country. He became known as the black golfer who nearly beat the Golden Bear. Six years later, after a host of similar near-misses and a controversial

Lee Elder at the Los Angeles Open.

trip to South Africa for a multi-racial competition at the height of apartheid, Elder was involved in another playoff—at the very place he had sworn off—Pensacola, site of the 1974 Monsanto Open. He was coming off a good showing at the Houston Open, so it wasn't much of a surprise to anyone when Elder birdied three of the final four holes to catch Peter Oosterhuis and force a playoff. Fellow tour members Hubert Green and Jim Wiechers maintained an open telephone line to Elder's wife, Rose, who had remained at the couple's home in Washington, D.C. Masters officials were apparently plugged in, too, because the ramifications of a black player winning a tour event and earning an invitation to the Masters were too huge to ignore. Elder seized the moment by ramming home an 18-foot birdie putt on the fourth extra hole to defeat Oosterhuis. Before the polite smattering of applause from the gallery abated, tour official Jack Tuthill grabbed Elder by the arm and, along with security, escorted him back to the same clubhouse he and the other black tour players had

"I'm the first, but I wasn't the pioneer. Charlie Sifford, Lee Elder, Teddy Rhodes, those guys paved the way for me to be here. I thank them. If it wasn't for them, I might not have had the chance to play here."

— Tiger Woods, after his Masters victory

been barred from six years earlier. "After I sat there for a while, I started thinking about what I had done," recalled Elder, whose picture hangs on the wall of the Pensacola CC clubhouse along with the other tournament champions. "Later I was told that Cliff Roberts called to congratulate me but I was at the 18th green for the awards ceremony." Elder would meet the chairman of Augusta National GC in person two months before the 1975 Masters when he, then-PGA Tour commissioner Deane Beman and another player were invited to play a practice round.

Roberts gave Elder a lukewarm reception on that occasion but was more gracious when Elder returned for the Masters. He met Elder's limousine, exchanged salutations with the golfer and his friend, Dr. Phil Smith, and led Elder to the registration site. The golf club's servants stopped what they were doing and stood in admiration as Elder walked by. "The blacks at Augusta were wonderful," recalled Elder. "They bent over backwards and did everything they could to show their appreciation for my qualifying and coming to Augusta. I'll never forget them."

Lee Elder at the 1975 Masters tournament. At the end of an exhausting week, Elder — not surprisingly — missed the cut.

The Elders rented two houses that week to throw the press off, and the ploy was effective for the most part. Still, the media crush was unlike anything Elder had ever seen. Publications and electronic news outlets that had only a passing interest in golf sent their best writers. "Jim Murray (of the Los Angeles Times) had been there only once, and he wrote a column saying he was going to the Masters because his good friend, Lee Elder, was playing," said Elder proudly. Lincoln Werden of The New York Times had a lot of private time with Elder. Ebony Magazine dispatched Pulitzer Prize-winning photographer Moneta Sleet Jr. to shadow Elder. He wasn't hard to find. Crowds followed him from the practice tee to the first tee each day. At 11:15 a.m. on April 10, Elder, paired with Gene Littler, laced a drive down the center of the first fairway at Augusta National. He never hit a more significant tee shot in his life. Elder shot 74, a pretty good showing amid all the distractions.

Paired with Miller Barber the next round, he shot 78 and missed the cut by four shots. He would play in five more Masters, making the cut in three of them. He had a career-best four-under-par 68 in the second round of the 1977 event and had his highest finish, a tie for 17th, two years later.

Elder's career took various twists and turns after that historic week in 1975. On the positive side of the ledger, he collected three more PGA Tour wins and more than $1 million in earnings. He also secured a place on the 1979 Ryder Cup team. He joined the Senior PGA Tour in 1984 and won $307,795 the next year to finish second on the money list. Between the tours, he has won more than $2.5 million. He has been one of the game's chief ambassadors, a friend to former President Gerald Ford and a humanitarian beloved for his philanthropic efforts, including the establishment of the Lee Elder Scholarship Foundation.

Elder has not, however, been immune to heartbreak. When Teddy Rhodes died, so did a piece of Elder's golfing soul. He and Rose had to relinquish management of Langston Golf Course in Washington, D.C., in the late 1980s because of financial problems. Shortly thereafter, they underwent a divorce that was anything but amicable. Elder suffered a mild heart attack in 1987 and hasn't been the same golfer since. A second marriage has been a life raft, he says. "My wife, Sharon, is the best thing that ever happened to me. She's my biggest supporter."

When Tiger Woods won the Masters, he said in his victory speech, "I'm the first, but I wasn't the pioneer. Charlie Sifford, Lee Elder, Teddy Rhodes, those guys paved the way for me to be here. I thank them. If it wasn't for them, I might not have had the chance to play here."

Back home in Chicago, Peggy White was overcome. "I cried like a baby when Tiger mentioned my father," she said. The legacies of Rhodes, Sifford and Elder are apparent—even through tears of joy.

Lee wins the Greater Hartford Open.

PGA of America

Lee Elder played on the 1979 Ryder Cup Team, captained by Billy Casper.

Comedian Flip Wilson with Lee and tournament director Bob Hope at the Bob Hope Desert Classic.

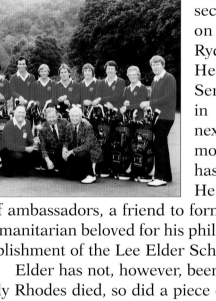

CHAPTER 9

TORCHBEARERS AND FLAMEOUTS

"I ain't afraid of nothing. I've taken chances all my life. If I get a chance to win, you can bet your ass I'm going to win." —Jim Thorpe

The fire lit by John Shippen and the other pioneers was anything but ephemeral. John Brooks Dendy, Robert (Pat) Ball and a host of other pre-World War II soldiers of misfortune stoked it. Teddy Rhodes, Charlie Sifford and Lee Elder fanned it. Others, such as Bill Spiller, were mere moths consumed by it.

"I understand Bill Spiller was a great player," said Jim Thorpe as he rolled one ball after another on the practice green at a Senior PGA Tour stop near Pensacola, Fla. "I never saw him play, but I understand he and Ted Rhodes were really something. I have a lot of respect for Charlie Sifford, too. I don't know if I could have endured what he went through. I think you have to be a certain kind of person to have that type of self-control. We've had a lot of great players, but the best black player, in my opinion, was a guy named James Black. He could do things with a ball that I never saw anybody else do."

If Sifford is golf's Jackie Robinson, Black is its Josh Gibson, a mighty force on the parallel circuit who never had a real chance to compete at the major-league level. Black was more the rule than the exception. The majority of African-Americans with potential saw Sifford's footprints in the sand but couldn't follow them. Some had flawed swings. Others had questionable character. A few couldn't find the first tee with a road map. For every Lee Elder there were two Chuck Thorpes, guys with a lot of game and even more hustle. For every overachiever like Jim Thorpe, there were two underachievers like Black. While Calvin Peete stands alone as one of the most accomplished African-American players, golf's back roads are littered with ne'r-do-wells, has-beens and wannabes. For every historic figure such as Pete Brown, there were dozens of players who were intimidated by their potential. That there have been only 26 African-Americans of record confirmed to have held a PGA Tour card (another handful were said to have been tour members but their claims are unsubstantiated) is hardly an aberration. When the final barrier was removed and people of color were allowed to play the tour, only a handful tried and even fewer converted the opportunity into prosperity. Most disappeared off the radar screen quicker than Haley's Comet. The

James Black in 1993.

Jim Thorpe was the first round leader at Merion in the 1981 U.S. Open. He went on to win three times on the PGA Tour.

stories of those who made it, as well as those who failed, form a rich tapestry with threads of delight and despair.

Two years after the PGA of America made Sifford a temporary approved tournament player in 1959, a young man who had caddied for Sifford in several PGA and UGA events, Rafe Botts, applied for a card of his own. Botts needed the signatures of two "Class A" PGA members in good standing on his application. While playing in a few West Coast tournaments, he asked Jerry Barber

> "I didn't look like a troublemaker. I knew how to do my fighting quietly, without making any waves."
>
> — Rafe Botts

(who was fresh off a playoff victory over Don January for the 1961 PGA Championship at Olympia Fields CC in Olympia Fields, Ill.) and his brother, Willie, to do the "honor." Jerry agreed to sign Botts' application, but when he found out that Botts had also gotten Willie to sign, he was livid. Recalled Botts, "He went berserk and wanted to take his name off. He felt one Barber in trouble with the PGA was enough. Jerry felt he had the name recognition to keep from getting kicked out of the PGA but that Willie might not." With support (albeit reluctant) from the Barbers, Botts received the small paper passport to the big time. Said Botts, "It was an approved tournament player's card, certainly not to be confused with a PGA membership card."

Jerry Barber, who helped Rafe Botts become a member of the PGA of America.

Botts' lifelong role as a bit player in major dramas began in post-war Washington, D.C., where he grew up. His father made gas mains for the Washington Gaslight Company in Georgetown and his mother was mainly a housewife, although she briefly took a job at the U.S. Department of Defense to help support Rafe and his 10 siblings. In 1949, 12-year-old Rafe hitched a ride to Langston GC with aspirations of assisting the family finances through caddieing. Too small to carry a golf bag, young Rafe was asked by one of the players to retrieve his practice balls. The shag boy earned 50 cents and his career in golf was launched.

James Black, Chuck Thorpe and Charlie Owens in 1970.

Two years later, he won a small trophy at a caddie tournament. It made only a small impression on the young ladies at Springard

High, though, who were smitten with the school's basketball star, a fellow named Elgin Baylor. Even then Rafe found it difficult to compete with those more gifted than him. Professional golf would prove no different.

Botts' game improved with practice and competition. One morning he made nine consecutive pars at Langston. Thrilled with the even-par score, young Rafe raced home to show the scorecard to his parents. "They weren't sports oriented," he recalled, "but they knew what I was trying to do. I had this overwhelming sense of wanting to be better."

Langston was home to some good players but none with the notoriety of Ted Rhodes and Joe Louis. When the duo showed up at Langston one day in the early '50s, young Rafe lobbied for their bags. Louis paid him $5 for nine holes, a small fortune in those days, and the caddie made a permanent connection between high rollers and high fades. However, his parents were high on education and before Rafe could chase his golf dream, he had to adhere to their academic expectations. A benefactor named Dr. Kenneth G. Brown taught Rafe more outside the classroom than he ever learned in it. Dr. Brown was a bone specialist on the staff at George Washington University Hospital. More importantly, he was president of the UGA in 1953-54. He took a liking to young Rafe and made him a traveling companion as he worked his way up and down the eastern seaboard overseeing UGA events. "He was one of the few black people who had real money, so he paid all my expenses," explained Botts. "I learned a lot from him. Just being around him, I learned how to interact with people. He used to tell me if I wanted something from people, I couldn't show them my angry face. 'You can't show them bitterness or you'll get rejection,' he'd say. It was a valuable lesson."

Rafe Botts, former UGA champion, who eventually competed on both the PGA and Senior PGA Tours.

With Dr. Brown's support, the tall, lanky Botts competed in the amateur division of UGA events, facing such stalwarts as Howard Brown, Joe Roach and Alfred (Tup) Holmes. When the Negro National Open returned to Langston in 1959, Botts parlayed his local knowledge into victory in the amateur division. The next day he left with Sifford for Southern California, a melting pot for aspiring African-American golfers in the '50s and '60s. Sifford lived near the Los Angeles Coliseum, where the Dodgers were hosting the Chicago White Sox in the World Series. Sifford's friend, Dodger second baseman and avid golfer Jim

(Junior) Gilliam, gave him a pair of tickets and Botts attended his first autumn classic. Just as Rhodes had been with him, Sifford was Botts' older brother in their quest to break into golf's establishment.

As a pro in 1960, Botts hung out at the Western Avenue GC, the legendary Los Angeles public course that spawned and nurtured so many talented African-American golfers, where a man's worth was often measured more by his heart than his golf skills. He and other West Coast-based players, including Sifford, Spiller and Rhodes, would play in local non-PGA sanctioned events such as the Gardena Valley Open, the Southern California Open and the Montebello Open, which were held in the off-season and frequented by many PGA Tour regulars. That's where he met the Barbers. "Jerry was a liberal if he liked you and he liked me," Botts said. "I didn't look like a troublemaker. I knew how to do my fighting quietly, without making any waves." On occasion, the water reached neck deep. During a PGA tournament at Lafayette, La., in the mid-'60s, Botts and Sifford overheard several men detailing how they intended to slice them up and serve them to the alligators in the Bayou. "That kind of stuff happened at a lot of places, mainly in the South," recalled Botts. "Sometimes they would get up and leave when we entered the dining room. You never felt comfortable. I was always a smiler, so, even though [the situation] was disturbing, I would just smile. Charlie used to call it 'Uncle Tomming.' I'd say, 'You look mean enough. If I look as mean as you, they'll kill both of us.'"

"I knew how to do my fighting quietly, without making waves." — *Rafe Botts*.

Botts' career, while unspectacular, mirrored his disposition. Even when he returned from military service in 1963 and had to jump through hoops to get his approved tournament player's card back, Botts remained quietly dignified. "When you go into the military, your old job is supposed to be held for you until you finish your tour of duty," Botts said. Apparently not with the PGA. "I had to reapply, so I got the signatures I needed and mailed it in with a return receipt requested. Somebody signed for it but it got lost. Eventually, I found out it was intentionally deep-sixed." Player committee chairman Bob Rosburg helped guide Botts through the proper channels and 90 days after he

Bob Rosburg.

© Jules Alexander

reapplied, Botts finally received his card. He never gained exempt status—Botts never finished higher than fourth in any tour event—but he withstood the uncertainty of Monday-morning qualifying until 1976. At the Sammy Davis, Jr.- Greater Hartford Open that year, Botts shot 69 in the qualifier to become first alternate. "I used to practice so hard that they'd ask me to leave because I would dig up the driving range," recalled Botts. "I'd get there at 7 in the morning and hit balls all day. I never had any formal training like Tiger Woods and Justin Leonard. I thought if I worked hard and really dedicated myself I'd be all right." After failing to make the field, Botts realized that all right was not good enough. He turned to good friend Lee Trevino for help.

> "White players on tour spoke very freely about how someday there would be a black player on tour who would be better than anyone else,"
>
> — Rafe Botts

"I told Lee I needed a favor, that I'd shot 69 and sat on the first tee all day and didn't get to play," recalled Botts. "I wanted to go home." Trevino took him inside the locker room, scribbled his name on a check and handed it to Botts. "He said, 'Here, this is not a loan, this is a gift. Have a good ride home, have a couple of drinks and I'll see you when I come out for the L.A. Open.' It was a check for $800. That's the kind of guy he was. We had an awesome relationship."

Botts played on the Senior PGA Tour from 1987-91 with similar results and has been a regular on the European senior circuit in recent years. He marvels at Tiger Woods' skill and proudly remembers that the coming of a player with Woods' ability was predicted decades ago. "White players on tour spoke very freely about how someday there would be a black player on tour who would be better than anyone else," Botts said. "Players like Julius Boros, Dow Finsterwald and Frank Stranahan believed that we had the rhythm, timing and elasticity in the muscles that were perfect for golf. I thought they were just placating me, but Tiger came along and proved them right."

As for Botts, the fact that he survived the harsh treatment and can still smile even after a wayward drive are satisfying accomplishments. "I didn't become a superstar because that wasn't my destiny," he said. "I know God had me exactly where he wanted me."

While more and more African-Americans were having an increasing impact on the nation's big three team sports—baseball, basketball and football—during the socially vibrant 1960s, their growth in the world of golf remained lethargic. As Sifford so eloquently put it in his autobiography, "Black players weren't looking for handouts, just equal opportunity." Just as Sifford and Botts waded into dark, foreboding waters, others locked arms and followed, among them Bill Wright, Howard (Lefty) Brown, Willie Brown, Cliff Brown, Gordon Chavis, Dick Thomas, Henry Baraben, James Black, Curtis Sifford, Al Green and James Walker Jr. The waters proved too deep for some, but Pete Brown was determined to stay afloat for as long as he could.

Brown's resolve was partly inherited from his father, a Mississippi sharecropper who taught himself carpentry and believed in the

> Brown's resolve was partly inherited from his father, a Mississippi sharecropper who taught himself carpentry and believed in the sanctity of soiled hands.

sanctity of soiled hands. Pete began caddieing at Jackson Municipal GC (now Edwin Guy GC) as an 11-year-old. "I watched those guys and they were so intense," recalled Brown. "A guy could play so bad one day and hit one good shot and that would make his day. He'd be back the next day. That intrigued me." He and some friends would occasionally "borrow" several clubs from the players for whom they looped and sneak on the course in the late afternoons for some quick competition. "We'd play for 15 minutes and run for 30, then come back and play again," said Brown. When Pete was 17, a local physician, Dr. John Davis, took him to City Park Golf Course in New Orleans, where African-Americans were allowed to play twice a week, on Mondays and Fridays. Two years later, in 1954, Brown entered the Lone Star Open in Houston, shot 292 for 72 holes, and finished second in the amateur division to Bill Spiller. The top black players competed for the pro purse, including Sifford, Moses Brooks, John Sanderson and Willie Brown, known for his prowess with the driver. "[Willie Brown] was the longest hitter in the world," said Pete Brown. "Jimmy Demaret and Jackie Burke used to bring guys in to Memorial Park to try and out-drive him but nobody

Charles Foster, one of the country's foremost trick shot artists. The native of Spartanburg, S.C., grew up in Detroit and served as an assistant professional to famed PGA member Ben Davis at Rackham Golf Club. Davis taught many of the top black touring pros and celebrities in the 1950s and '60s, including Joe Louis. Foster had an 11-year stint as national golf clinic representative for Lynx Golf, Inc. He continues to conduct a creative and entertaining clinic across the country.

ever could." Shortly after the good showing in Houston, Pete turned pro and got a multi-faceted job at Edwin Guy GC. He was the caddie master, locker room attendant and course superintendent, all for $30 a week in salary. "Sometimes I would sneak and give some of the ladies lessons," he said. He won the Lone Star in 1955 and wound up in Detroit the next year working as a desk clerk at the Garfield Hotel and Lounge, owned by Randolph Wallace, a black businessman from Mississippi. Wallace offered to fund Brown's college education in return for his services as a golf instructor for his family. But two months after the move, Brown was in a Detroit hospital engaged in a fight for his life.

Brown was stricken with non-paralytic polio, a disease that caused him to lose control of his muscles, but at first doctors were unable to make the diagnosis. He felt ignored, a patient of low priority in the segregated facility. "They gave me up for dead," Brown said. "The doctor told me if I did survive I'd have to give up golf because I'd be in a wheelchair the rest of my life." Joe Louis and Sifford visited Brown, but his condition had worsened to the point that he was unable to recognize or acknowledge them. "They left an autographed picture on my bed," Brown said. "That's how I knew they had been there. The doctor saw the picture and told me I must be an important guy to have Joe as a friend and they started treating me better." Brown was bedridden for 11 months, but slowly, through stringent physical therapy, he began to recover. Within months of his release, Brown resumed his golf career as head pro at Grove Park GC, a public course owned and run by the city of Jackson mainly for African-Americans. A year later, in 1958, he returned to Detroit and competitive golf.

Brown won the 1961 Michigan Open at Farmington CC after shooting 67 the morning of the final round before the leaders had even teed off. Never suspecting his score would land him in a playoff, Brown found some libation and a hill with a view. When the announcer summoned him to the first tee for the playoff against Tom Targeton, he was "slightly" inebriated. "I could barely stand up," he recalled, laughing at the memory. He managed to halve the first hole with a par, then two-putted for a winning birdie at the second "that shocked the whole state." Wallace, Brown's financial advisor and backer, sent him to Los Angeles to gain the experience he would need to advance to the next level—the PGA Tour. Sifford convinced Class A pros Jimmy De Voe of Fox Hill G&CC and Earl Martin of Western Avenue GC to sign Brown's approved tournament player's application. He received his card in July of 1963.

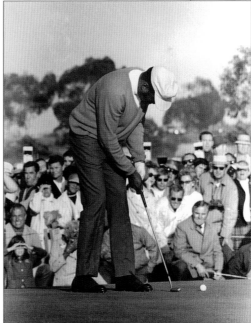

Pete Brown, whose win at the 1964 Waco Turner Open was the first by an African-American in a PGA Tour event.

Brown quickly rose as a competent player on tour and his performance at the Waco Turner Open in Burneyville, Okla., in the spring of 1964 further distinguished him as a worthy competitor. He shot 68 in the third round to get into contention, then played somewhat conservatively in the final round. He didn't look at a scoreboard until he putted out on the 17th hole. When he did he was surprised to see that he had a one-shot lead on Dan Sikes. "I knew if I parred 18 victory was mine," recalled Brown. His prospects dimmed when he pulled his 2-iron tee shot at the 230-yard par-3 into the rough. But Brown flopped the ball to three feet and calmly sank the putt—becoming, on May 3, the first African-American to win a PGA-sanctioned tournament. "At the time, I didn't think much about it," said Brown, who won $2,700 in official prize money and another $340 in bonus cash. "It hit me that night and I didn't know how to handle it. I started thinking about all the opportunities it would open up for me, like the Tournament of Champions. But I didn't think about the Masters, because I knew I wasn't going there."

> … Brown flopped the ball to three feet and calmly sank the putt—becoming, on May 3, the first African-American to win a PGA-sanctioned tournament.

Brown earned $21,796 that year to finish 29th on the PGA Tour money list. But, as he suspected, an invitation to the 1965 Masters the following spring was not forthcoming. "I played good enough in '64 to get in," Brown said, "but, really, neither me nor Charlie [Sifford] ever met their qualifications. They really didn't want Charlie there because he had raised so much hell. Cliff Roberts told me they didn't want to invite a black because they didn't think we'd accept charity. I didn't think much of the tournament anyway because it had the weakest field in golf." Brown won a second event, the Andy Williams-San Diego Open, in February of 1970 to once again put himself in position for a Masters invitation (in those days, the tournament used a point system to determine who qualified for the field). But a 75 in the final round at Doral derailed his trip to Augusta. "The Florida swing was the key," he said. "I would have qualified but for that 75." Still, he won a career-high $56,069 that year. A few years later, back problems, the residue from his bout with polio, forced him off the tour. After a short stint on the Senior PGA Tour, Brown took over as full-time head pro at Madden GC in Dayton, Ohio, where he has been ever since. "I never really learned how to walk right after being hospitalized and I couldn't run at all," he said. "I never was really right after that. There's no telling how good I could have been, but I'm grateful for the time I had on

James Black, Tournament Director Charles Collette and local pro Ted Tipton at the Sky View Open at Asheville Municipal Golf Course. Black won the event.

tour." So are those who came after him.

Pete Brown was already an established member of the PGA Tour when a fellow Southerner named George Johnson emerged from one of two qualifying schools in 1968, along with three other African-Americans—Nathaniel Starks, James Walker Jr. and Curtis Sifford, Charlie's nephew. It was the beginning of an era in which (counting Monday-morning qualifiers and the occasional African-American Class A pro who made it into a tournament field) the tour became resplendent with people of color—at least compared to the way it had been throughout the 1940s, '50s and most of the '60s. Between 1969 and 1980, there were as many as 10 full-time African-American members of the tour in any given year. Johnson ("G.G." to his friends) was one of the most talented.

The third oldest of six children born to George Sr. and Johnnie Mae, George admired his parents, both mill workers in Columbus, Ga., whose calloused hands kept bread on the table and a steady beat during Sunday church service. George Sr. was a Baptist minister. Young George might have leaned that way, too, had it not been for some high school friends who coaxed him into caddieing at the Lion's Club course and later the Columbus CC. Within a year, George and his friends carved three holes of about 150 yards each from a nearby field. He'd hit 5-irons late into the evening, until his hands blistered. "I only had that one club, but I could hit almost any shot with it," recalled Johnson. "I'd challenge anybody to come over and play."

George Johnson qualified for the PGA Tour in 1968.

Johnson left Columbus for Atlanta in 1962, a raw talent with a winning personality. After impressing the regulars at Lincoln CC, the club's management decided to back him in African-American mini-tours—the so-called chittlin' circuits mostly along the east coast. Traveling with Starks and fellow Atlantan Carl Seldon, Johnson became a regular on both the United Golfers Association and North American Golf Association tours. But it was a tournament run independently of either organization that gave Johnson the best idea of what it must be like on the PGA Tour. "The North-South in Miami was the best-run tournament we had," Johnson said. "Ray Mitchell (who founded the event in 1954) was just a great guy who knew how to organize and get sponsors. He did a lot for us, gave us a place to play and really encouraged the growth of the game among blacks." Most of the great African-American players stopped by Mitchell's playground on their way to the show. Johnson used the North-South as a catalyst for his most dominating year on the black tours, 1967, when he won four consecutive tournaments. That's when he decided it was time to try the PGA Tour.

His first two years on tour produced indifferent results, marred by the resistance he encountered in the events he played in Memphis, Pensacola and other southern cities. He'd had a taste of the unpleasantness he was to face a few years earlier in a U.S. Open qualifier at East Lake GC in Atlanta. After finishing his round, one of his playing partners, East Lake member Charlie Harrison, invited him inside the grillroom for lunch. Johnson reluctantly joined him. That one gesture of friendship nearly cost Harrison his membership. Only Harrison's request for support from the club's most revered member, Bobby Jones, kept offended East Lake members from expelling Harrison. Johnson never knew a corned beef on rye could cause so much trouble.

George Johnson today.

The racial incidents he endured in Memphis and Pensacola still leave him with a queasy feeling in the pit of his stomach. "We had a hard time getting through security check points," said Johnson, whose Afro hairstyle and bell-bottom pants symbolized freedom of expression and a threat to the status quo. "We didn't have any identification or player's cards, so they thought we had to be caddies." Johnson never got used to the bigotry but did eventually become acclimated to the various courses and competition by his third season. In 1971, he defeated rookie Ralph Johnston on the first hole of a sudden-death playoff to win the Azalea Open, a satellite event at Cape Fear CC in Wilmington, N.C. He would never win again, although he had four runner-up finishes over the remainder of a career that spanned 10 years. "I'm proud I was able to stay out there that long," he said. "It wasn't always easy, but I have some fond memories, too. I remember teeing it up with Nicklaus and Trevino. I played with Jack in the third round of the Canadian Open in the mid-'70s. We both had 138 the first two rounds. And I played with (major league baseball catcher) Johnny Bench in the Crosby for about four years running. Even made a hole-in-one at No. 7 at Pebble Beach one year."

Johnson tried the Senior PGA Tour as an alternate for a couple seasons in the early '90s but hand problems forced him to retire from competitive golf and accept a job as head pro at Bobby Nichols GC in Louisville. He never earned more than $40,000 any year on tour, but his perseverance inspired future millionaires.

By all accounts, James Black should have been one of them. "At one time, I thought I was the greatest player in the world," said the Charlotte (N.C.) native. "The game of golf and I were like one." Black might have been the first African-American golf prodigy. He discovered golf as an eight-year-old caddie at Bonnet Brae GC, a public track off limits to minorities. The game quickly supplanted his first love, baseball. The low-income housing development where Black lived was like most other urban prisons of that period: It had one way in and out. Black and some of his buddies who lived there dug holes in the paths between the cookie cutter buildings and inserted cans in them. Miniature golf, ghetto style, proved a big hit. "We knocked out a lot of window panes," said Black, laughing at the recollection. "We also started to get pretty good at it. A lot of white golfers started to recognize my talent." One of them, a local fireman and member at Carolina CC named Horace

> Black might have been one of the first African-American golf prodigies. He discovered golf as an eight-year-old caddie ...

Phillips, was Black's regular bag at Bonnie Brae. One morning, Black, feeling pretty cocky, told Phillips that he could beat the fireman without breaking a sweat. The next week, on caddie play day at Bonnie Brae, he proved it. "Next thing you know, he's telling one of his friends that I could beat their best ball," recalled Black. "After I did that, they started bringing in golfers for me to play. They made all the money. I was 13 and pretty good."

In retrospect, the seed of unfulfilled potential might have been sewn during those gambling matches. James Black the tournament player never outplayed James Black the hustler. At 15, he advanced to the quarterfinals of the amateur division in the Negro National Championship at East Potomac Park GC in Washington, D.C., before losing to a player 10 years his senior. Two years later, he won the Negro National Junior title. The silver trophy he received was nice, but even more thrilling was meeting some of the black role models who were in attendance that week, including Jackie Robinson, Joe Louis, Sugar Ray Robinson, Larry Doby and Don Newcombe. "I used to walk around with my head down," said Black, "but Jackie Robinson told me to keep looking forward because I was a champion early in life and champions hold their head up high. That was a great message for me."

His skill caught the attention of Sam Snead in the mid-1950s during one of Snead's junkets to North Carolina. PGA Tour star Vance Heafner invited Black to play at his club, Eastwood in Charlotte. Ten minutes into Black's pre-round workout on the practice tee, Heafner was convinced that Black was the real deal. "He told me I had a great pair of hands and feet," Black said.

Black turned pro in 1962 and hit the black tours, winning the UGA national championship twice. His brashness was like a shot of straight whiskey to some of the veterans. At the 1964 Los Angeles Open, he gave the mainstreamers a glimpse of what Snead

Curtis Sifford, Charlie's nephew, played sporadically on the PGA Tour in the 1970s.

reported back to his fellow tourists as "a colored boy with some kind of golf game." One of the more clever Los Angeles headline writers described his first-round 67 that tied Roger Ginsburg as "The Deacon and the Rabbi." The Deacon eventually finished in a tie for fifth that week behind winner Paul Harney. He qualified at Mimosa CC in Morganton, N.C., for the U.S. Open later that year and set his sights on playing the PGA Tour in 1965. One of Black's earliest

> One of the most spirited, though short-lived, rivalries on the black tours involved Black and a sharply-dressed Floridian who gripped the club cross-handed and had a noticeable hinge in his left knee.

benefactors was North Carolina senator Herman Moore, who gave him $250 a week in financial support to help bankroll his career. But six months into Black's first season, Moore's payments ended. "I was on my own after that," remembered Black. "It was pretty much the beginning of the end." By the end of the year, Black was back on the chittlin' circuit. This time, unlike the tenement in which he grew up, there was no way out. He would dominate the black tours, winning dozens of titles. But he would never again return to the PGA Tour.

Black eventually returned to Charlotte and maintained his connection with the game by establishing a junior golf program for inner-city youths called Project M-E (motivation and education). "Golf is the ultimate self-help sport," he said. "It's different from any other in that there is no one to help you win. It's a great character builder. It requires creativity and imagination. I believe in giving at-risk kids an opportunity to play a non-traditional sport like golf. I'm committed to teaching them the benefits beyond those you see on TV. In a small way, I believe I can help change things."

One of the most spirited, though short-lived, rivalries on the black tours involved Black and a sharply-dressed Floridian who gripped the club cross-handed and had a noticeable hinge in his left knee. Charlie Owens didn't need an introduction to golf fans on the Florida winter tour or to those on the UGA circuit. But when he came to Asheville, N.C., in the late 1960s to play in his first Skyview Open, he was a stranger to long-time followers of the NAGA. He flashed his credentials with three consecutive sub-par rounds to tie Black and officially launch their

*Golfers wait out a rain delay at the 1969 Sky View (left to right): **Harry Jeter**, **Arthur Gilbert**, **Carver Thorpe**, **Jimmy Wesley** and **Bobby Stroble**. James Black would go on the win the '69 tournament.*

*Sam Snead, shown here with **Bobby Jones**, "discovered" James Black in the mid-1950s in North Carolina.*

rivalry. Black won this first battle with his legendary "devil's dream" wedge approach shot on the first playoff hole. The ball sailed over a stand of pine trees in the right rough about 50 yards short of the green and took a 45-degree turn left, landing on the putting surface some 20 feet right of the hole. As if drawn by a magnet, the ball spun toward the cup, stopping 24 inches away. Owens congratulated Black warmly; he could accept defeat graciously because he had been in tougher fights throughout his entire life.

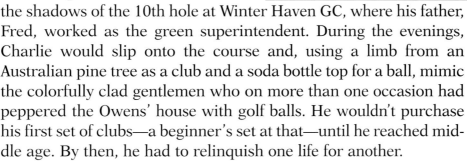

Charlie Lee Owens grew up in Winter Haven, Fla., during the Great Depression. He was born in the shadows of the 10th hole at Winter Haven GC, where his father, Fred, worked as the green superintendent. During the evenings, Charlie would slip onto the course and, using a limb from an Australian pine tree as a club and a soda bottle top for a ball, mimic the colorfully clad gentlemen who on more than one occasion had peppered the Owens' house with golf balls. He wouldn't purchase his first set of clubs—a beginner's set at that—until he reached middle age. By then, he had to relinquish one life for another.

Chuck Thorpe with his wife, **Susan**, after winning the Sky View Open in 1981.

"I shot 67 in a caddie tournament when I was 14 years old," Owens said. "After that, I consistently shot in the 60s. There weren't many white players around who could beat me, but no white courses we could play on."

Charles Owens overcame severe knee injuries to become a scratch-handicap golfer and a champion on the UGA circuit.

Owens was in his third year at Florida A&M University on a football scholarship when he was inducted into the military. After serving for the 82nd Airborne in Korea, he was discharged from the Army in 1953 and returned to Winter Haven, where he got a job driving for the city bus line. But when he was harassed by a white driver on his first day of training, Owens decided the front lines held less danger than the home front and re-enlisted. This time an accident during a training exercise changed the course of his life forever. He suffered a broken knee parachuting from a plane, which immediately ended his military career.

Owens bounced from one job to another until finally settling in as an assistant manager at a sporting goods store in New York. The pain in his knee was so unbearable, he decided to have bone-muscle fusion surgery. Though it relieved the pain, it severely limited his flexibility. Owens, 37, lay in his Brooklyn hospital bed and confronted reality—he had little money and even fewer prospects. "I could see guys playing the Dyker Beach course from my window, and my heart suddenly longed to be out there," recalled Owens. "I hadn't touched a golf club for nearly 20 years, but I felt the game was still in me." Within a week of being released from the hospital, Owens was playing $5 Nassaus at Dyker Beach. Shortly after

that, he purchased that beginner's set of clubs and a Sunday bag from a Kroger's sporting goods store for $20 and began a relentless practice schedule. By 1967, his game was sharp enough for him to enter UGA events in New York, New Jersey and Connecticut. "A lot of them were one-day tournaments," Owens said. "The wives would cook and, after the tournament, we'd eat and drink in the parking lot. First-place money was from $300-500. I won enough one summer to drive a Cadillac and stock its trunk with a dozen pairs of pretty shoes. Then I met a guy named Dave Rosen, who was probably the first Nevada Bob. He gave me my first real set of golf clubs—a set of MacGregors—a lizard golf bag and six or seven pairs of shoes. I was wearing custom-made shirts. I was one of the best-dressed dudes you ever saw."

Though his PGA Tour was marred by health problems, Owens would go on to win twice on the Senior PGA Tour.

In 1968, Owens won eight of the 13 UGA events he entered, then migrated south to play the Florida winter tour, competing with future PGA members such as Bruce Fleisher, Bruce Lietzke, Sam Adams and Gibby Gilbert. The next year he qualified for the PGA Tour along with another African-American, Jim Dent, and Hubert Green, Rik Massengale and Buddy Allin. Wilson signed him to a $10,000 endorsement deal. "I thought there was no stopping me," he said. Barely keeping his card the first two years on tour, Owens finally broke through in a satellite event, the Kemper Asheville (N.C.) Open, in 1971. The rigors of the tour, however, proved too much for his knee, which was operated on several more times. He was an infrequent member of the tour much of the 1970s because of health problems. However, the worst was yet to come. At the 1977 Sammy Davis Jr.-Greater Hartford Open, he was standing over a putt in the second round when his hands started to shake. It marked the onset of the yips, which were a constant source of embarrassment from then on. They drove him to construct and experiment with long-shafted putters. Quite possibly the first "name" player to use one in competition, Owens bounced back to become a successful member of the Senior PGA Tour in the 1980s, winning twice in '86 and earning nearly $800,000 in his senior career. He received the Ben Hogan

Award in 1987 and was later inducted into the Florida Sports Hall of Fame.

Lee Elder.

By the time Owens returned to Charlotte in 1991 for Arnold Palmer's tournament, the PaineWebber Invitational, his right knee was nearly as uncooperative as the left had always been. His vision was so bad in his left eye that he played mostly by feel. A few miles away, James Black preached the lessons of golf and life to a group of eager youths. The two players' paths had not converged since those halcyon days on the alternate tour, but it provided them a wonderful memory.

Jim Dent and Chuck Thorpe were also big names on the black tours during the 1960s and early '70s. Only Elder and Black might have had more marquee value than Thorpe, second oldest of five golfing sons of the Roxboro (N.C.) GC greenskeeper. Thorpe's golf game was only surpassed by his charisma. "He's always been a good-looking man, a ladies man," said his younger brother, Jim. "Hell, Chuck must have been married a half dozen times." Chuck got his PGA Tour card in 1972 but failed to keep it. From then on, he was a permanent fixture on the mini-tours, except for the occasional appearance in a PGA Tour event. Chuck was blessed with talent far beyond his much more successful brother, Jim. However, he never made the connection between heart and head. Said Jim, "Two stories pretty much sum up my brother. I was playing in a tournament in Newport News, Va., back in the '60s. Chuck was hitting balls on the practice range, drawing a big gallery, because Chuck could really pipe it. Arnold Palmer was standing there talking to my Daddy. Palmer pointed at Chuck and said 'Mr. Thorpe, there's a million dollar's worth of talent but that brain he's got might not be worth 10 cents.' Another time, Chuck was leading the L.A. Open. When the reporters asked him how it felt to be leading, he crossed his arms, flashed a smile and said, 'Hell, I didn't come to Hollywood to win no tournament; I came to be a movie star.'"

Chuck Thorpe won the Sky View Open six times.

Chuck Thorpe qualified for the Senior PGA Tour in the mid-'90s and played it sporadically for the rest of the decade. But he never rose above the hand-to-mouth existence of the various mini-tours and, thus, never attained what should have been his rightful place among the best African-American players ever. "In life, there's a time for everything," said Jim Thorpe. "What bothers me most is that God gave Chuck a second chance—the senior tour— and he never took advantage of it. I've learned a lot from watching Chuck. I've learned not to make the same mistakes."

Dent was quietly watching Chuck Thorpe self-destruct, too, determined not to squander his considerable talent. While Thorpe drew criticism for a lack of work ethic, James Lacey Dent grew up in Augusta, Ga., with a grinder's mentality and focus. Dent was always big for his age and superbly skilled as an athlete. He played football for Lucy Laney High alongside the school's best all-purpose player, Emerson Boozer, who later enjoyed a celebrated pro career with the New York Jets. Dent caddied at both Augusta National GC and Augusta CC, where a locker-room attendant nicknamed "Bodiddly" gave him a golf club and showed him how to use it. Like almost every other African-American golfer who eventually made it to the PGA Tour, Dent's road there wound through small southern towns with law enforcement officials far less amiable than Andy Taylor. He shared sleeping quarters in flophouses with his chittlin' circuit brethren. In 1966, Dent took $40 of the $200 he had saved, bought a plane ticket to Los Angeles and set out to join several black tour refugees, including Curtis Sifford and James Walker Jr. He moved into a one-room apartment at $60 per month and started hanging out at Western Avenue GC. Moses Stevens, financial backer of several other black players, decided to stake the long-hitting Dent. Four years later, he graduated from the tour's qualifying school.

Like many big hitters before him, Dent had a poor short game. That flaw, more than anything, kept him out of the winner's circle his entire career on the regular tour. The closest he came to victory was a tie for second in the 1972 Walt Disney World Classic, won by Jack Nicklaus. He lost his tour card in 1985 and again in '87, then dedicated the better part of two years to shoring

George Simkins, Gordon Chavis, Lee Elder, Perry Shitsett, Murphy Streat and Sam Edwards at a tournament in the 1950s.

Jim Dent, who once caddied at Augusta National, became a PGA Tour regular — and one of the most prolific winners in Senior PGA Tour history. During his PGA Tour career, Dent was considered the longest driver in the game.

up his short game in preparation for the senior tour. He worked with famed instructor Jimmy Ballard, but the pieces finally came together through tips from future fellow senior tourists Lee Trevino and Dave Stockton. It didn't take him long to parlay those lessons into victory. In the final round of the 1989 MONY Syracuse Senior Classic, Dent eagled the 17th hole to take a one-shot lead over Dick Hendrickson. Facing a six-footer for par at the 18th, he fought to hold his emotions in check. When the putt dropped into the cup, Dent blew away a lifetime of doubts with one, loud exhale. "I had been out there 18 years and finally found out what winning was all about," he said. "I can't describe the pride I felt. It put my name up in lights. I realized winning is everything. If you don't win, they forget about you."

They wouldn't forget about Jim Dent. He made sure of that. Through 1999 he had won 12 times on the Senior PGA Tour (13th on the tour's all-time list) and amassed more than $7 million in earnings. But the man nicknamed "Big Boy" by his fellow seniors had an even bigger impact on the game among people of color in this country. "I've been accepted, made a lot of money and had a lot of fun," Dent said. "Have I gotten the respect I deserved? I don't know. But what can we do about it? You go on about your business and don't let it bother you." Jim Dent went about his business better than most.

While Dent's prodigious drives brought him notoriety and marketability, a famous name helped Jimmy Lee Thorpe capture public attention. Besides a moniker, the other thing Jim Thorpe the golfer had in common with Jim Thorpe the American sports icon was an unquenchable thirst for being in the mix. "I'm not afraid of anything," said Thorpe the golfer. "I've taken chances all my life. If I get a chance to win, you can bet your ass I'm going to win." Thorpe got that chance four times in his 24-year PGA Tour career and was successful in three of them. The lone exception was at the 1985 Western Open at Butler National GC outside Chicago when he lost a playoff to amateur Scott Verplank but still collected first-place money. His doggedness was forged from a father's toughness and the absolute joy he got from proving skeptics wrong. "I remember one time my brothers and I were run off Roxboro Golf Course," recalled Thorpe, the ninth of 12 children. "My Daddy told the pro, 'Dammit, if my boys are good enough to work on this golf course, they're good enough to play on it.' Nobody ever said anything to the Thorpe boys about playing on that course again."

A star athlete at Person County High, Thorpe received a football scholarship to Morgan State University in 1967. But golf

A weak short game stymied Dent's PGA Tour career; as a senior, his improved touch has helped earn 12 wins.

was in his blood and shortly after his football career ended, he turned his attention to the fairways. He got married and settled in Virginia, close enough to the action on the public courses of Washington, D.C., and Baltimore that his wife, Carol, knew their head pros by name. She worked for HUD; he worked at East Potomac Park and Langston in D.C. and Clifton Park in Baltimore, and any-

> Thorpe was an aggressive player with an unorthodox swing that resembled a lumberjack cracking a whip.

where else he could get a game. He hustled—and sometimes got outhustled—by the best black players on the East Coast, guys such as Jimmy Wesley, Earl Robinson and George (Tater Pie) Wallace, a black-tour legend who shared the name George with eight other family members, including famous comedian brother George Henry Wallace. At first, Thorpe's talent didn't match his ambition. He could hit it into the next area code, but couldn't always find it. When he told his caddie friend Richard (Jelly) Hansberry of his PGA Tour aspirations, Hansberry warned him against it. "He said, 'You aren't ready,'" Thorpe said. "I trusted his opinion. So I decided to get ready. Every day for six weeks, I hit balls way back behind some pine trees at Pine Ridge Golf Course in Baltimore. When I came out from back in those trees, my hook didn't hook anymore. I could find it." He first attempted the qualifying school in 1975, but didn't succeed until 1978, when he was co-medalist with John Fought. By then, Thorpe

PGA Tour/Stan Badz

Jim Thorpe (above and at right) possesses a very athletic, yet somewhat unorthodox, swing. His ability to consistently drive the ball in the fair-way is a large part of the reason his record in the U.S. Open is so strong.

had developed an appetite for horse breeding and racing. He once cashed in on a trifecta worth $62,000. Like most gamblers, Thorpe also suffered some heavy loss-es. "In '85 when Verplank won but I [got first-place money], I think I signed that check and sent it to a casino," he said, laughing. "But I never took any money out of the household. I only gam-bled with what I called my 'mess up money'—the money I got for a corporate outing or pro-am."

Thorpe was an aggressive player with an unorthodox swing that resembled a lumberjack cracking a whip. On a mid-June morning in 1981 in Ardmore, Pa., the lumberjack took a big divot out of one of golf's biggest trees. The 66 he shot in the first round of the U.S. Open at Merion GC proved significant not because he was the first African-American to lead an Open—John

© PGA Tour/Chris Condon

Shippen had earned that honor 85 years earlier—but because television cameras recorded it. For one day, a black golfer had scaled the mountain and the world had witnessed it. "Sure, it was a helluva accomplishment for a black man," Thorpe said, "but what I remember most was that I was leading the U.S. Open and I couldn't buy breakfast the next morning. I had just bought a new house in Buffalo and all my credit cards were maxed out. My wife called me that night and congratulated me on leading the Open. Then she asked me why I hadn't taken any money with me. I told her not to worry, that I'd be OK. There was some cereal and milk and fruit in the locker room, and that's what I ate. Looking back, it was one of the greatest things that happened in my life."

Thorpe couldn't sustain that caliber of play for 72 holes at Merion and wound up tied for 11th. But he fulfilled his promise. He won nearly $2 million on the PGA Tour, then primed himself for the Senior PGA Tour, determined to make more of his second chance than his brother, Chuck. "I've made a lot of friends out here," he said. "I've done all right financially. Except for that one time [at Roxboro], I've never had a negative experience."

Almost unnoticed in that U.S. Open was another African-American who arrived with little fanfare on the world golf scene by finishing a shot back of Thorpe. Calvin Peete shot 67 in the third round and closed with an even-par 70 to tie Lanny Wadkins and finish ahead of such luminaries as Tom Watson, Johnny Miller, Raymond Floyd and Curtis Strange. Peete's quiet ascension in the Open, a championship that demands accuracy and course management, foreshadowed his decade of dominance.

Calvin Peete was the tour's most accurate player during the 1980s. In all he won 12 tournaments on the tour.

Peete's path to professional golf began in Detroit and wound through every migrant farm worker camp from Pahokee, Fla., to Rochester, N.Y. He was picking cherries among the migrants in Sutton Bay, Mich., in 1955 when a tree limb snapped, sending him crashing to earth. He landed on his left elbow, shattering it in three places. He was never able to completely straighten the arm again. Orthopedic surgeons advised that re-breaking and resetting it probably wouldn't correct the problem. "I decided to leave it alone," Peete said. "The only time I really worried about it was when I got into golf." Instead, the fall would eventually elevate him to unprecedented heights.

In 1958, Peete and a couple of teenaged friends left Pahokee in search of adventure and manhood. Each had various skills. Peete played pool with the kind of astuteness developed through many hours of truancy. He would accept with a self-assured nod the challenge from those who thought they had a better stick, then offer words of consolation to the vanquished. But it was his enterprising nature and ability to talk himself out of a tight spot that separated Peete from the pack. He obtained a wholesale peddler's license, purchased imperishable goods like clothing, housewares and jewelry, and sold them from the trunk of his car to migrant workers. It proved a profitable business to the young man. "I was making about $150-200 a week, pretty good money at the time [in the 1960s]," recalled Peete. "By the time I was 25 years old, I had $250,000 worth of real estate in Fort Lauderdale."

By then, he had also discovered golf—a new frontier with endless possibilities. Some friends talked him into playing nine holes with them at Genessee Valley Park GC in Rochester. "I was hooked from the moment the club hit my hand," Peete said. "I watched a bunch of hackers dribbling the ball off the tee and thought to myself, 'I think I can learn this game.'" He was 23 and hungry for a new competitive outlet, and golf was a perfect fit. Six months later, he entered the North and South at Miami Springs G&CC in Miami. A 76 qualified him for the championship flight, and even though he wouldn't break 80 the final two rounds, his first foray into competitive golf confirmed his natural ability. His first thought was to follow his pool-hall instincts. "I saw dollar signs walking around in alpaca sweaters," Peete said.

But before he could get swept into the current of misguided perspective, fate intervened. He was sitting inside the clubhouse at Orange Brook GC in Hollywood, Fla., one day waiting out a thunderstorm when he caught a glimpse of the television broadcast of a PGA Tour event. There on the TV screen was Lee Elder, engaged in a sudden-death playoff with golf's golden icon, Jack Nicklaus. Peete couldn't take his eyes off the screen. "I watched this man play about four or five holes before Jack finally won," recalled Peete. "I was so impressed with his game from tee to green, his mannerisms, his professionalism. At that moment, I wanted to be like Lee Elder." He realized that in order to emulate Elder, he had to improve his work ethic and alter his lifestyle. He began pounding balls from sunup until sundown at a public park in Fort Lauderdale and playing marathon matches against himself. "I thought if I worked at it, within a few years I'd be out there with Lee," Peete said. "It didn't happen that

Peete won the PGA Tour's flagship event, *The Players Championship*, in 1985. At the time, it was the most significant win by an African-American.

© PGA Tour

quick, but in about six years, in 1972, I turned pro."

That was the easy part. Peete gave himself a narrow window of opportunity, five years, to make it or try something else. He played in the National Tournament Golfers' Association series of mini-tour events around Tampa, did well enough to

Racism threw a few glancing blows at Peete, but few landed. "Sifford, Elder, Brown and Dent really paved the way for me," he said. "I was pretty much accepted as a player."

boost his confidence, then decided to try the PGA Tour qualifying school in the fall of '72. Three years later, on his third attempt, Peete got his card by finishing eighth in a class that included Bruce

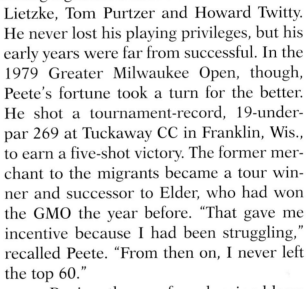

Lietzke, Tom Purtzer and Howard Twitty. He never lost his playing privileges, but his early years were far from successful. In the 1979 Greater Milwaukee Open, though, Peete's fortune took a turn for the better. He shot a tournament-record, 19-under-par 269 at Tuckaway CC in Franklin, Wis., to earn a five-shot victory. The former merchant to the migrants became a tour winner and successor to Elder, who had won the GMO the year before. "That gave me incentive because I had been struggling," recalled Peete. "From then on, I never left the top 60."

Peete teamed with **Ben Crenshaw** at the 1983 Ryder Cup.

Racism threw a few glancing blows at Peete, but few landed. "Sifford, Elder, Brown and Dent really paved the way for me," he said. "I was pretty much accepted as a player." He would have been difficult to overlook. He won 11 times in the '80s, including four triumphs in 1982 and the 1985 Tournament Players Championship, and collected the Vardon Trophy for low stroke average in 1984. Only Tom Kite won more often during the decade and no one drove the ball more accurately. The guy with the crooked arm was the tour's straightest hitter every season from 1981-90. He was a member of the winning U.S. Ryder Cup team in 1983, and the losing U.S. team two years later, the first American side to lose in the event in 28 years.

Peete (front right) and the rest of the victorious 1983 U.S. Ryder Cup team.

By the end of the decade Peete's name appeared less often on leader boards. Rumored reasons ranged from the predictable to the absurd—from complacency to suspected substance abuse. In actuality, the heart of his problems was a failed marriage, which plunged him into a deep depression. "The divorce (in 1986) was devastating," he said. "Also, each stage of my life was keyed around setting goals and reaching them. Once I reached that mountaintop, I had no more goals."

The 1985 Ryder Cup team, captained by Lee Trevino, marked Peete's second appearance in the event.

PGA of America

Peete also suffered a series of injuries. He faded from the regular tour, leaving Thorpe the only African-American to continue what Sifford started. Peete resurfaced on the Senior PGA Tour in 1993 but the embers had but a faint glow. "In the '80s, I think I was over-golfed," Peete said. "I don't have much incentive to play, but I'd like to get healthy and maybe win again. I'd like to finish well. I think my golf speaks for itself. They'll remember me because they can't burn the books. It may be so far back there that you'll need a magnifying glass to find it, but they can't write me out."

Peete proved African-American players could not only compete but excel at the highest level. Two others, Bobby Stroble and Walter Morgan, proved that for some, life begins at 50. Stroble won nearly 120 tournaments as a journeyman who saw too many backwater towns and too little green. The Albany, Ga., native turned pro in 1967 and was relegated to life on the mini-tours for much of his career, primarily because of an inability to earn, and keep, his PGA Tour card. He qualified for the big leagues three times in the 1970s and '80s but managed less than $5,000 in total earnings. The Senior Series, a mini-tour for players prepping for the Senior PGA Tour, proved much more profitable. Stroble won $85,000 on that circuit in 1994, then qualified for the senior tour a year later. Through 1999, he had banked more than $1 million. However, his life has not been without several distasteful detours, including a four-month-long stint in prison for interstate transportation of stolen property. "That's life," said Stroble. "I welcome some curves. Anybody can hit a fastball."

Walter Morgan, in competition on the Senior PGA Tour, with his trademark cigar.

© PGA Tour/Stan Badz

Morgan was career military but knew nothing of former Army golf standouts Charlie Sifford, Murry Jacobs and Tex Guillory. He had grown up as a baseball fanatic in Haddock, Ga., and pursued that interest in the military. While stationed in Hawaii in the late-1960s, he wandered over to a driving range near the base-ball field and started hitting golf balls. In 1975 and '76, he captured All-Service honors. Upon being discharged in 1980, Morgan lined up a job as the club pro at a course at Fort Hood, Texas. He played in numerous PGA section and mini-tour events around Texas, then, approaching 50, told some friends at Fort Hood of his intentions to give the Senior PGA Tour a try. "There were a lot of guys who told me I couldn't make it, but I guess I proved them wrong," he said. In his fourth full season on tour, Morgan put himself in position to win the 1995 GTE Northwest Classic. The friendly fire he faced from playing partners and fellow qualifying school classmates Bruce Summerhays and Bob E. Smith was nothing compared to the all-out assault from contenders Dave Stockton and George Archer in the group ahead. "Each time they would do something good, I'd do something good," recalled Morgan. He did a lot of good that day, winning by three strokes and several smoke rings from an ever-present cigar. "A week or so later, when I really thought about what I'd done, I had chills," said Morgan, who would win two more tourna-ments and more than $3 million by the end of 1999.

In April 1999, eight African-American graybeards gathered at the Senior PGA Tour stop near Pensacola, Fla., including Jim and Bill Thorpe—the first time two African-American brothers had qual-ified for a PGA event. The gathering was in silent celebration of all the faces that made even the briefest appearance on the major tours. Players such as Rafe Botts, Pete Brown, Howard (Lefty) Brown, Cliff Brown and Adrian Stills (who had the distinction of being the last African-American to qualify for the PGA Tour, in 1985). None of them won that week, but their presence was a minor victory in itself. On the other side of Florida, the world's top players tussled over a multi-million-dollar purse. Only one of them, Tiger Woods, was a person of African-American descent. Said Jim Thorpe in 1994, "When I first came out on the PGA Tour, there were eight or 10 black players here. Now, 18 years later, I'm the only one left. And in five years, when I go to the Senior PGA Tour, there probably won't be any." One torch, one hand, one lonely stretch of history.

Bobby Stroble has won more than $1 million on the Senior PGA Tour.

© PGA Tour/Stan Badz

CHAPTER 10

FIRST IMPRESSIONS

"I didn't even answer. I just hung up. As far as I was concerned I was a golfer, just like any other, and that's how I'd been treated. I wasn't going to let anything spoil the moment." —1959 U.S. Public Links champion Bill Wright

With renewed confidence quickening his pace, Tiger Woods strode to the 38th green at Pumpkin Ridge GC near Portland, Ore. He managed a slight smile as the gallery acknowledged his arrival. He was about to stick his head above ground for the first time after clawing his way out of a six-foot-deep hole. The fresh air was revitalizing and rarefied.

Steve Scott, a University of Florida freshman with industrial-strength toughness, surveyed his short flop shot to the par-3 green as Woods feigned nonchalance. Scott had conjured up a miracle in a similar situation earlier that day in his attempt to deny Woods an unprecedented third consecutive U.S. Amateur championship. Another shovel full of dirt would surely bury Woods for good. Scott's pitch and subsequent par putt both missed their mark, leaving Woods a tap-in from golfing immortality. He emerged from the premature internment a nascent folk hero, second only to Bobby Jones as this country's greatest amateur golfer.

Within a fortnight of his threepeat, Woods, unfathomable fortune to go along with global fame just a signature away, turned professional and began the next stroke in a historic work in progress. Back home in Southern California, William A. (Bill) Wright and Alton Duhon, two graying former national champions, felt the connection between past and present. Wright, the first African-American player to successfully negotiate the rough terrain between junior golf on an interracial level and a USGA title, received little acclaim for his victory in the 1959 USGA Amateur Public Links. So, too, did Duhon when he won the USGA Senior Amateur 23 years later. Woods collected converts because of kinder, gentler times and because his accomplishments were pinned on golf's future like medals of valor. Earlier that year, when Eddie Payton-led Jackson State University became the first historically black college to receive a berth in the NCAA Division I Championships, the expedition to unexplored territory took another small step. Payton had only two African-Americans among his starting five, but they symbolized the long journey to validate the position of non-whites in the game. It is a struggle all too familiar to Harold and Jeff Dunovant, the only

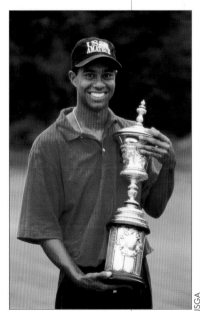

*1996 U.S. Amateur champion **Tiger Woods**.*

William A. Wright, 1959 U.S. Amateur Public Links champion.

African-American father-and-son members of the PGA of America. Jeff played at Fayetteville State. Harold attended Winston-Salem State University. While Woods' success was trumpeted by thousands, that of Wright, Duhon, Payton and the Dunovants drew little more attention than a distant drum in a hail storm. The marks they made on history, however, are undeniable.

> Wright wasn't spoon-fed surlyn from the time he could consume solids, so he doesn't exactly qualify as the first African-American test-tube golfer.

Unlike Woods, Wright wasn't spoon-fed surlyn from the time he could consume solids, so he doesn't exactly qualify as the first African-American test-tube golfer. However, he did develop tremendous skill in the game with only a brief stint in the caddie yard. That, and the fact that both of his parents were golfers, made him unique among his contemporaries. His father, Bob, was a postal worker who moved the family from Kansas City to Portland and finally to Seattle when Bill was 12. Madeline, his mother, was an elementary school teacher and social worker and the perfect balance to Bob's tough love. When young Bill would complain about the fickle Seattle weather, Bob's comeback was always the same. "It never rains on the golf course, son," he would say. The Wrights lived near Jefferson Park, the same public course where Fred Couples would later learn the game. One day, Bill decided to tag along with his father to examine this meteorological miracle for himself and found the wonders of metal striking ball instead. A couple years later, while his parents were petitioning the State of Washington to open all of its public courses to people of color, young Bill was posting low enough numbers at Jefferson Park and West Seattle GC to qualify for the City Amateur. "When I went to play in the tournament," recalled Wright, "the sports editor of the *Post Intelligencer*, who was also the tournament director, asked me [to get] off the tee." It was 1950, five years prior to the Supreme Court ruling that prohibited discrimination at public facilities, and the Wrights had neither the political nor the financial clout to challenge the discrimination in the legal system. However, they quietly protested, enjoyed their family golf outings and watched young Bill develop as a two-sport star (golf and basketball) at Franklin High, a school with a handful of minorities and no apparent racial problems. As a tall and lanky power forward, Wright led Franklin to the city championship in 1954. He played with future Los Angeles Lakers star Elgin Baylor in Amateur Athletic Union competition during the summers and further positioned himself for a

Eddie Payton, former NFL defensive back and brother of Walter Payton, is the coach of the Jackson State University golf team.

Jackson State University

college scholarship, which, unfortunately, never came. Forced to walk on in both basketball and golf at Western Washington College, he soon encountered Jim Crow lurking in the halls of higher learning. The NAIA school practiced and played its home matches at Bellingham CC, a private club that also made its facilities available to the local high school and junior high golf teams. When word spread that Western had an African-American on its team, Bellingham CC officials threatened to sever their relationship with all outside parties, Western Washington in particular. Club officials relented only when Wright agreed to practice at a shabby public course outside the confines of Bellingham and to set foot on club grounds only for scheduled matches. "By my senior year, though, I was pretty much accepted all over Bellingham," he said.

Basketball great **Elgin Baylor**, *AAU teammate of Bill Wright, who would go on to make sports history of his own.*

Acceptance as one of the country's top amateur golfers came a lot easier. Wright developed enough of a reputation in college to announce his presence as a force among small-school competitors on the West Coast. Charlie Sifford and many of the Los Angeles-based professionals were familiar with Bob Wright's son. Sifford and the elder Wright played regular matches whenever Sifford would come to Seattle as part of Billy Eckstine's entourage. Bill would caddie for his father, who more than held his own, and occasionally showed off for the visitors. However, when Wright finally qualified for the USGA Amateur Public Links at Wellshire GC in Denver in 1959, his name didn't exactly strike fear into the hearts of his fellow competitors. But by the time he reached the final match, long after tournament favorite and defending champion Dan Sikes Jr. had been dispatched, the quiet young man with the magical putting touch had created quite a buzz. "He was the only person who out-putted me in a match in my life," said Don Essig III, recalling with admiration Wright's 23 one-putt greens and gentlemanly behavior in their 36-hole semifinal match that Wright won, 1 up. "I've been beaten by better players but I've never been beaten by a finer gentleman."

Wright's decorous demeanor withstood a little gamesmanship by his opponent in the final, Frank Campbell, of Jacksonville, Fla. Fellow competitor Cliff Brown, one of the handful of African-American qualifiers in the field, had warned Wright about Campbell's veiled tactics. "Cliff was from the South and he said he used to caddie for Campbell," Wright said. "He told me to beware of Campbell saying things to try to get me off my game. Hell, I wasn't from the South, so I didn't have a clue as to what he was talking about." He found out on the first hole, a par-5 that he had birdied every round. This time, however, Wright skulled his tee shot and was forced to lay up on his second. Campbell's drive split the fairway, and he appeared to have an advantage after his second shot rolled onto the fringe of the green. "What do you think about that, son?" Campbell said, smiling. Wright didn't respond, but he replayed Brown's warning in his mind. A pitch and a putt later, Wright had jumpstarted his round with another birdie. Meanwhile, Campbell took three to get down from the fringe. "That's what I think about that," Wright said as the pair exited the green. "It doesn't matter how you drive it, it's how you finish it."

Wright's short game bailed him out whenever his long but erratic driving found a tenuous lie. At the 33rd hole, he sliced a drive inches from out-of-bounds, then punched a low-flying 8-iron between some tree limbs and onto the apron of the green. Two putts later, he closed out the match, 3 and 2. Most of the estimated 2,500 onlookers graciously acknowledged the new champion. Wright shook Campbell's hand, and the tree of opportunity, simultaneously. Accolades fell sweetly on his shoulders. "It was a proud moment for me, a great experience," Wright said. "I was treated very well, not one bad incident." A telephone call from a reporter at the *Post-Intelligencer* interrupted Wright's post-victory celebration. "The first thing he wanted to know was if I had received any flak from anyone associated with the tournament about my being the first black champion," Wright recalled. "I didn't even answer. I just hung up. As far as I was concerned I was a golfer, just like any other, and that's how I'd been treated. I wasn't going to let anything spoil the moment."

Wright's success stretched into the next year, as he won the NAIA individual title and a City Amateur crown. As a 24-year-old college graduate with an impressive list of golf accomplishments in one hand

William A. Wright in action in the 1959 National Public Links Championship.

and a degree in the other, he had many options and a bright future. His first choice was to attempt a pro golf career. But in order to do that, Wright needed funds and his bank account was empty. Fiercely independent, he only half-heartedly sought sponsorship. In 1961, after exhausting the few leads he had on financial backing, he and wife Ceta moved to Los Angeles and took jobs as elementary school teachers. By 1964, the Wrights had put away

$2,000; that summer Bill drove to Hartford, Conn., for his first pro tournament—the Insurance City Open. "I remember Charlie Sifford and Pete Brown being there and Charlie asking me where I was staying," Wright said. "I told him I was staying at a hotel overlooking the Hilton. I was actually staying at the local YMCA. Almost every week I was on tour I stayed at the same hotel overlooking the same Hilton." Three years of inactivity had little effect on Wright's competitiveness. He opened with a 69, then shot 68-67 to get into contention. Paired with 1963 U.S. Open winner Julius Boros in the final round, Wright suffered a meltdown from which he never really recovered. He would spend the next 12 years playing the PGA Tour, with little success. After retiring, Wright went on to enjoy a lucrative career in the private business sector before eventually returning to golf in another capacity. Since the early '90s, he has been teaching the game at The

Alton Duhon, 1982 U.S. Senior Amateur champion, another product of the famous Western Avenue Golf Club in Los Angeles.

Lakes at El Segundo, a nine-hole course near the Los Angeles International Airport. Most of his pupils know nothing of his past. And he prefers it that way. "Golf is a sport that has no appeal to anybody," Wright says. "It's a quiet sport. It's intrinsic. It's not something you shout about. There's a feeling inside you that cannot be duplicated in any other sport."

Alton Duhon resisted the giddiness of golf when a co-worker first took him out for a round in the spring of 1950. He had moved to Los Angeles after a tour of duty in the Navy. Nothing on the playgrounds of Lafayette, La. (where he was born and reared), or in the regimen of service, prepared him for the diabolical nature of the game. "I quickly decided this is not for me," recalled Duhon, detailing his day of frustration. Another co-worker at Zenith Plastics baited Duhon into giving the game another try by providing him with a set of clubs. At the end of the round, the co-worker had a daily playing partner—and golf another convert. Duhon lived on 120th Street and Avalon, just up the street from Bill Spiller. He would watch Spiller hit balls in the field behind his house and marvel at his graceful swing. Later, as his game developed, Duhon became a respected player around Western Avenue GC. Even Spiller and the L.A. community of black pros who played out of Western took note of his skill. Duhon, though, never strayed from the amateur ranks, playing mostly in Southern California. The Western States Golf Association, a black amateur organization that spreads westward from Arizona, proved fertile ground for Duhon's domination. He won numerous WSGA titles but, more importantly, gained the experience he would need in the national arena. His gut told him that's where he belonged. "My father tried to become the president of a black union back in the South but he got fired for trying," Duhon said. "The Duhon name never rung loud, but I was determined to [change that]."

> "I came here to win, that if I qualified, I'd win. I'd make history. I just knew it."
>
> — Alton Duhon

He qualified for the U.S. Amateur a few times but never advanced past the opening round of match play. But once he reached the senior amateur ranks, it was another story. In the 1982 USGA Senior Amateur at Tucson (Ariz.) CC, the 57-year-old Duhon was determined to validate his career and said as much in a pre-tournament interview. "A newspaper reporter asked me what I was doing there," Duhon said. "I said, 'I came here to win, that if I qualified, I'd win. I'd make history.' I just knew it." After a come-from-behind, 3-and-1 win over 1973 champion William Hyndman III in the quarterfinals, the field knew his intentions, too. When he defeated Dick Giddings, 7 and 6, in the semifinals, Duhon became only the second African-American player (and the first since Wright) to play in the final match of a USGA championship. With a piece of history in his hip pocket, Duhon took on defending champ—and Tucson CC member—Ed Updegraff for the title. "There must have been 3,000 in the gallery and every time he'd win a hole, they'd holler," said Duhon, recalling Updegraff's home-club advantage. "I won a couple holes early to go 2 up, then he won 8 and 9. But when I birdied 14 to go back up, the party was pretty much over." Any chance Updegraff had to extend the match disappeared with Duhon's stake-in-the-heart, 35-foot birdie putt at 18. When the ball tumbled into the hole, Duhon raised both arms in victory as if to salute his father. The Duhon name rang loudly in press accounts from coast to coast.

Duhon turned pro in 1988 and tried the Senior PGA Tour, but made little impact. He retired from competitive golf in 1996 and started a junior golf program at Chester Washington GC in Southern California. Every Sunday after church, the former champ pitches the lessons of golf and life to about two dozen disadvantaged youths. "I'm trying to give them something I didn't have: help," he says. "I want them to do better than me."

While Duhon basked in the glory of his national title, Eddie Payton studied the tendencies of the NFL's top pass catchers and running backs, including those of his brother, Walter, a future Hall of Fame halfback and stalwart for the Chicago Bears. Eddie was in the final quarter of a successful football career himself, one that began in Columbia, Miss., and would eventually reach the

Metrodome in Minnesota, home of the NFL's Vikings. As an NFL player, Eddie was never able to escape the colossal shadow of his famous brother. But when he arrived back in Jackson, Miss., where he had starred for Jackson State University, Payton started to cast a pretty big shadow of his own. A.F. Smith, the school's longtime golf coach, was retiring. Athletic director Dr. Walter Reed asked Payton, an avid golfer who had once considered a professional career, if he'd take over the program. "I was looking for a way to get back into the university and golf was a perfect fit," Payton said.

The Jackson State University golf teams.

Jackson State University

By recruiting the top African-American talent in the country, Payton instantly transformed Jackson State into an emerging power among historically black colleges. However, he had bigger plans for JSU. The Southwest Athletic Conference championship trophy made a good conversation piece but Payton wanted to build a program worthy of national recognition and that meant an upgrade in talent and schedule. "Bob Brown of the University of New Orleans was the first white coach to invite us to his tournament [in the 1987 season], and we finished pretty bad," recalled Payton. "It exposed our weaknesses. Bob gave me some great advice. He said that if we wanted to compete, we had to integrate. If not, we were going to have to try and overcome the reputation that historically black teams had established: that we couldn't play, lacked discipline and wouldn't show up if we were invited. So we integrated the next year."

It took Payton eight more years to find the right combination of players. But in 1995 a Jackson State team anchored by Tim O'Neal, an All-American from Savannah, Ga., cracked the top 25 in several major college polls. While O'Neal, an African-American, was clearly the star, a trio of starters—Aussies Mike Brennan and Craig Hocknull, plus white player A.J. Montecinos—proved major contributors and sources of controversy. Payton vehemently defended his team's racial mix. "It's unfair of people to criticize Jackson State for recruiting white players," he said. "We're only doing the same thing that the Oklahomas, Nebraskas and UNLVs have been doing for years in football and basketball. Nobody says anything when the majority of their teams are black. It's no different with us in golf."

Payton's team might have scored points with the pollsters, but the NCAA selection committee had ignored JSU two years running, despite Payton's politicking. The following spring, several national publications detailed Payton's plight. In May, Jackson State earned a berth in the Midwest Regional, becoming the first historically black college to compete in the NCAA Division I championships. Although JSU placed 15th at the University of Michigan GC in Ann Arbor and failed to advance to the finals, Payton's efforts cast historically black colleges in a new light. "We accomplished one of our main goals at Jackson State and every player that has ever teed it up for us was a part of that success," Payton said. "No one can ever take that away from them. There can only be one first; there can be many to follow, but history remembers the first."

Dunovant established the National Black Golf Hall of Fame in 1986 to recognize the contributions of African-American players to the game. Induction ceremonies are held annually in conjunction with a pro-am at Bel-Aire GC in Greensboro.

Perhaps it was Harold Dunovant's bellicose attitude that kept him forever standing on history's doorstep. His family moved from Winston-Salem, N.C., to New York when Harold was a teenager but not before he had been branded by Southern shepherds. "There were so many places we couldn't go and things we couldn't do," Dunovant said. "It was like being fenced in. When I got to New York and found out black people could play golf legally at the Van Cortlandt course in the Bronx, it was like I had been set free." Dunovant turned pro in 1954, and, like all the other aspiring African-American players, found a home on the UGA. "I made money everywhere I went, but I was a very poor putter and that kept me from being as good as I could have been," Dunovant said. In 1960, he began a campaign to become the first African-American Class A teaching professional. Fourteen years and numerous run-ins with the PGA

Harold Dunovant, Herman DuBois and Jimmy Taylor, UGA player representatives in the 1965 North-South Open.

of America later, he finally became a Class A member as head pro at Winston Lakes GC in Winston-Salem. "It had been the toughest journey in the world," he said. "For years wherever I went, from the Metropolitan Section to the Carolinas Section, they wouldn't accept me. But when I could finally pull out that piece of paper and show them I was a full-fledged member, they had no choice but to accept me."

Dunovant established the National Black Golf Hall of Fame in 1986 to recognize the contributions of African-American players to the game. Induction ceremonies are held annually in conjunction with a pro-am at Bel-Aire GC in Greensboro. The faces of black golf are remembered each year around Independence Day, thanks to one who refused to let his be forgotten. However, the Hall of Fame is only part of Dunovant's legacy. In October of 1993, his son, Jeff, followed his father's path and joined the PGA of America as a Class A teaching pro. "I had more pride in Jeffrey getting his card than when I got my own," Dunovant said. "I felt like a pioneer when I got mine, but when he got one, too, I felt like all the heartbreak had been worth it."

In 1999, the Carolinas Section of the PGA honored Harold Dunovant as its junior golf leader of the year. With the recognition, another African-American golfer's long journey into day was finally complete.

*North Carolina native **Harold Dunovant**, an African-American pioneer within the PGA of America, established the National Black Golf Hall of Fame in 1986.*

CHAPTER 11

BEYOND THE CREEK
AND THROUGH THE WOODS

"The problem is that black people are prejudiced against dark-skinned people, so it's no surprise that white people are, too."
—John Merchant, former USGA executive committee member.

Beginning with John Shippen's unpopular appearance at the U.S. Open in 1896, the thawing process between African-Americans and golf in this country seemed cyclical. About every three decades something or someone would chip off another layer of icy relations and, at worst, reveal a platform for peaceful coexistence and, at best, one for significant change. In 1925, a group of businessmen began the United Golfers Association, for which every person of color who has earned one dime of PGA Tour earnings should forever be grateful. Thirty years later, a Georgia union shop representative led a non-violent revolt that opened public golf courses to all Americans, regardless of race or gender. And nearly three decades after the PGA of America's notorious "Caucasian-only" clause was rescinded, the infamous Shoal Creek incident pushed golf back on its heels. Industry magnates and, more importantly, corporate America, finally became enlightened to the plight of African-Americans in the game. Once the stone found its mark, the ripple effect was predictable. Blacks started showing up in the most unexpected places. The USGA appointed John Franklin Merchant to its executive committee. William (Bill) Dickey, a retired real estate and insurance executive who had dedicated his life to providing educational opportunities for minorities through golf, suddenly had the ear of college presidents and athletic directors. Joe Louis Barrow Jr., son of boxing great and golf barrier breaker Joe Louis, rose to an executive's position for a fledgling golf company. He would ascend even higher in the golf industry by the new millennium. Country clubs extended invitations of membership to blacks of means. The game's governing bodies not only started to subsidize programs aimed at inclusion but they began to initiate them as well. Blacks, in limited numbers of course, started showing up on their payrolls. Golf would never be the same.

Merchant had an augury of his destiny as a graduate stu-

PGA of America

Bill Dickey *received the PGA of America's Distinguished Service Award from the organization's CEO,* ***Jim Awtrey*** *and his wife.*

John Merchant, *the first African-American member of the USGA's executive committee.*

USGA

dent at the University of Virginia when he looked around and saw only one black face: his. A native of Greenwich, Conn., Merchant would go on to become the first African-American graduate of the U-Va Law School. "I entered Virginia the year after Brown vs. the Board of Education," said Merchant, who had completed undergraduate studies at Virginia Union. "There were a lot of battles being waged on various battlegrounds. [James] Meredith was marching to

> ... the thawing process between African-Americans and golf in this country seemed cyclical. About every three decades something or someone would chip off another layer of icy relations and, at worst, reveal a platform for peaceful coexistence and, at best, one for significant change.

Mississippi. I, for one, was not trying to draw any attention to myself." He was able to blend in at Virginia during turbulent times on the campuses of other Southern universities because of a lack of skin pigmentation and a load of self-confidence. "I won't deny that being light-skinned made things easier," Merchant said. "It still does. The problem is that black people are prejudiced against dark-skinned people, so it's no surprise that white people are, too."

John Merchant, walking fairways as a USGA referee at the 1993 U.S. Open at Baltusrol Golf Club.

After law school, Merchant fulfilled an obligation to serve his country with a tour of duty in the Navy. While stationed in Hawaii, he was introduced to the game that would alter his life. Fellow officer John Richardson, a 5-handicap from Birmingham, Calif., took Merchant to the Navy/Marine course. Merchant shot in the triple digits but was buoyed by encouraging words from Richardson, who believed, with some lessons, Merchant could become a good player. After balking at the necessity of instruction, Merchant bet his friend $50 that within six months he would break 80 without benefit of a single lesson. Eighteen weeks later, he collected his winnings.

John Merchant presiding over the trophy ceremony at the U.S. Senior Amateur Championship.

Upon being discharged from the Navy, Merchant returned to Connecticut, where he started a law practice and chased golf balls around public playgrounds. Never a shrinking violet, Merchant navigated this country's rough political waters in the '60s and '70s with poise while keeping an eye on the national landscape. Much

Sandy Tatum (left), past president of the USGA. Jerry Tarde (right), editor of Golf Digest.

of what would become his ideology came from watching the successes and failures of others. Said Merchant, "When the civil rights movement reached its stride, it never really had a philosophical orientation. It was an expression of anger and outrage against negative treatment that had been and was continuing to be imposed upon us. Martin Luther King was the only guy who had a vision to bring about change. And he understood that change would be incremental and take time." Merchant's "time" came the summer after the discontent caused by the Shoal Creek flap. He received a telephone call from friend and colleague Giles Payne. Payne was an advisor to USGA past-president Frank D. (Sandy) Tatum Jr., who was serving as chairman of the nominating committee for prospective members of the executive committee. As a result of Shoal Creek, and partly inspired by a column written by *Golf Digest* editor Jerry Tarde challenging the USGA, the organization sought to diversify. Payne believed Merchant was an obvious candidate to become the first African-American member of the committee in the 97-year history of the USGA. During a two-hour meeting, Merchant impressed Tatum, who in turn told USGA president C. Grant Spaeth the good news. In January of 1992, Merchant integrated the 16-member executive committee.

It didn't take him long to push an agenda that had first been proposed by Rose Harper-Elder to Tarde. Harper-Elder thought that a symposium, bringing together industry leaders and persons interested in growing the game, would be the first step toward diversifying golf. Merchant took the lead in developing the concept and ran with it. "I wanted to begin the process of building a responsible, well-respected organization that could interface with the power system in golf, so that doors could be opened, when possible, for blacks to get involved in golf at all levels. Not just playing on the tours but in every aspect of the industry." He took the proposed symposium to the executive committee. "I told them I was going to do it no matter what," he said. "I said, 'If it succeeds, you can take credit for it. If it fails, fire me.' I was hoping they would support it, but I was

Leroy Richie, the first African-American to serve as general counsel of the USGA.

determined to do it anyway." Financed by Golf Digest and the USGA and coordinated by Golf Digest managing editor Lisa Furlong, the Minority Golf Symposium convened at Callaway Gardens, Ga., in the fall of 1992. Tennis legend and civil rights activist Arthur Ashe was among the invitees but failed to show. It might have been the only negative from that initial meeting, one in which, for the first time, people from different backgrounds held an open dialogue about the game's future. Out of the symposium (which met four more times) grew the National Minority Golf Foundation, the umbrella organization for all others involved in every aspect of the game impacting minorities, from junior golf to business. The USGA voted in 1996 to fully fund the NMGF, with Merchant as its president and chief executive officer, for three years. Within the organization's first year, Merchant was deposed. The man who served four one-year terms on the USGA executive committee and also acted as Tiger Woods' legal counsel when the latter turned professional, returned to private law practice. "I had the vision," Merchant said. "If you look back to January of 1992 when I first went on the executive committee, there were very few black people—if any—who could talk to important people in the golf world as equals. Today, when you see people like Craig Bowen [director of the National Minority Golf College Scholarship Fund] and Joe Louis Barrow, they are an indication that my vision was correct."

> On encountering the PGA's 'Caucasian-only' clause at the 1952 San Diego Open, "They can tell me to my face that I can't play."
> — Joe Louis Barrow to his son
>
> Blacks were not looking for a handout, no special rules and no special dispensation. They just wanted a level playing field.
> — Joe Louis Barrow Jr.

So was Bill Dickey's. In fact, Dickey and his organization, the National Minority Junior Golf Scholarship Association, headquartered in Phoenix, were very much a part of Merchant's big picture. Leroy Richie, the first African-American to serve as general counsel for the USGA (1992-97), convinced Merchant in 1995 that the symposium should incorporate the NMJGSA and allow Dickey to get some staffing support. However, it never went from concept to reality and Dickey, an ageless wonder, has continued to be the glue of an organization that has donated nearly a million dollars to minority student-athletes.

Dickey grew up in Philadelphia and was a major-league baseball prospect before getting sidetracked by a stint in the Air Force. He moved to Phoenix after being discharged, completed a degree in economics and management from Arizona State University in 1956 and fell in with a group called the Desert Mashie Golf Club. In 1983, he founded the NMJGSA, which tracks the progress of minority golfers between the ages of 13-18. The purpose was to provide scholarships so students could obtain a quality education while playing golf. The NMJGSA receives most of its funding from the annual East-West Golf Classic and uses some of its proceeds to support black college golf programs. Dickey's dedication has been responsible for the steady proliferation of African-Americans in various segments of the golf industry. "It's been a labor of love," said Dickey, who in August 1999 received the PGA of America's Distinguished Service Award for his contributions to the game. "Just to know that I've played a small role in helping young minorities fulfill their potential is very rewarding. We still have a long way to go, though. The fight is not over."

Attendees at the first Minority Golf Symposium, financed by the USGA and Golf Digest, *in 1992.*

The fight was in Joe Louis Barrow even before he knew it. Joe was born in Mexico City and grew up a celebrity's kid in Chicago. His parents divorced when he was young, but Joe remembers the quiet times with his father in high school and college—most of which were on the golf course. "That's when I really got to have intimate, warm conversations with him," Barrow said.

Barrow was reared by his mother and stepfather on the south side of Chicago, in a neighborhood called Hyde Park. He was a member of the golf team for the University of Chicago Laboratory High School but couldn't play Jackson Park, the public course within walking distance of his home, until his senior year. One of Barrow's most vivid childhood memories involves a golf outing with his father, Teddy Rhodes and Althea Gibson. An opportunity to spend a day with his father usually so excited young Joe that the night before brought little sleep. When his father's sedan rumbled into the driveway that morning, Joe, clubs slung over his shoulder, rushed out the door to meet it. The two of them

Panel members at the Minority Golf Symposium: **Steve Mona** *(GCSAA),* **Lisa Furlong** *(Golf Digest),* **Tim Finchem** *(PGA TOUR),* **Mike Moraghan** *(U-Va Golf Coach) and* **Joe Beditz** *(NGF).*

were engaged in small talk as they passed Jackson Park. Suddenly Louis grimaced as if absorbing a body blow. There was little conversation the remainder of the hour-long drive to Pipe O' Peace Golf Course, the city-owned layout where minorities were welcomed. Pipe O' Peace was renamed Joe Louis The Champ Golf Course in the early '90s, but the vibration from that body blow never left Barrow, not even when segregation died at Chicago's other public facilities.

> Because of the perseverance and determination of those who fought to level the lie, it is now less difficult for the nearly one million African-Americans who play the game to make it.

"The reason blacks were eventually able to play Jackson Park is because the neighborhood around it became more integrated," Barrow said. "The South Shore neighborhood had been mostly white but when blacks moved in, most of [the white people] moved out."

Barrow inherited his father's love for golf, which, in turn, enabled him to understand the passion that drove men like Teddy Rhodes and Charlie Sifford. Rhodes was "Uncle Ted" to him and a steadfast friend to his father. Barrow was only 5 when his father became the first African-American to play in a PGA Tour event—the 1952 San Diego Open. "The sponsors invited him, not realizing there was a Caucasian-only clause on the PGA," Barrow said.

Compliments Joe Louis Barrow Jr.

*Ted Rhodes, Joe Louis and Joe's son, **Joe Louis Barrow**, now head of the First Tee Program.*

"He went to San Diego and said, 'They can tell me to my face that I can't play.' Blacks were not looking for a handout, no special rules and no special dispensation. They just wanted a level playing field. Blacks knew they had the ability and skills. They just wanted an opportunity to play."

The stumbling blocks were apparent even to a child of privilege. So was the humanity exhibited by some individuals who found ways to help Louis and others leap over those blocks. Louis told his son stories about the benevolence of Bob Hope and Bing Crosby, fair-minded men with whom the champ played many rounds of golf. When they played courses that prohibited African-

Joe Louis Barrow (left) and *John Merchant*, two of the leading African-Americans on the administrative side of the game.

Americans from entering the clubhouse, Crosby and Hope would run interference for Louis, demanding that their playing partner be treated with the same amount of respect as anyone else. Their kindness touched Louis, whose son devoured the tales about genuine heroes in a game whose stewards were seldom made of similar sturdy stuff. "There's no question in my mind that there was a great deal of interest [among African-Americans] in golf when I was growing up," Barrow said, "just like there was a great deal of interest in baseball, with the Negro Baseball League. If blacks had been able to enter golf simultaneously when Jackie Robinson was entering baseball, I think there would be a lot more blacks playing golf today."

Barrow graduated from the University of Denver in 1968, had a stint as senior advisor to Ron Brown at the Democratic National Committee in D.C., then returned to Denver, where he was swept up in the current generated by Shoal Creek. In 1992, he was invited to join segregated Denver Country Club. In May of 1994, his application was approved and he became the club's first African-American member. "We didn't explicitly talk about Shoal Creek during the process," he said, "but there was a very strong sense that the time was right and it was necessary for Denver Country Club to expand its membership." Ironically, it

Earnie Ellison of the PGA of America staff.

was only a short time later that Barrow found himself in a position of power within the golf industry. A friend of his was handling marketing and public relations for an upstart golf bag strap manufacturer named T.J. Izzo and recommended Barrow as a viable recruit to the team. Said Barrow, "T.J. is the inventor of the product. He, a Spanish woman named Georgina Drummond and I started the company [Izzo Systems Inc.]. The fact that I'm in the golf industry has

Craig Bowen.

nothing to do with the fact that I'm black but everything to do with the fact that I'm a marketing professional."

Barrow also is a man on the move in the industry. In January of 2000, he was named director of The First Tee, the World Golf

Foundation's initiative designed to get minority and disadvantaged children involved in the game. He also was appointed chairman of the National Golf Foundation. The positions give Barrow a rare opportunity to affect change. "It is my chance to make a difference," he said.

> "I think my father would be pleased there are no rules precluding African-Americans or any minority from playing on the PGA Tour."
>
> — Joe Louis Barrow Jr.

Barrow, Dickey and Bowen are three of a handful of high profile African-Americans in the industry. Earl Woods, president of Tiger's foundation, and Earnie Ellison, Director of Diversity Programs of the PGA of America, are two others, as are Barbara Douglas, president of the National Minority Golf Foundation, and Julius Mason, director of public relations and media relations for the PGA of America. More have infiltrated the rank-and-file, but they are mere window dressing for the decision-makers. "It's not evidenced by people having affirmative action or open recruiting policies," said Barrow. "The success of the industry should be evidenced by the number of African-Americans, women, Hispanics and Asians there are in key positions with an organization. If you have that criteria, then you can do the analysis."

Even though the number of golf industry executives is few and the only faces of a dark hue found in professional golf are but a few years short of retirement, the analysis is not as bleak as it appears. Martin Luther King knew that change would be incremental. The struggle requires small steps, like a boxing champion cutting off an opponent in the ring. "I think my father would be pleased there are no rules precluding African-Americans or any minority from playing on the PGA Tour," Barrow said. "That was the first hurdle he and the other blacks of the '30s, '40s and '50s faced. That barrier no longer exists. Today, making the tour is the by-product of an individual's skill and interest. And that, I think he would say, is a matter of time and energy. If people have it in their gut to do it, they ought to do it. The burden of proving one's self is now on the individual, just as my father had to prove himself. He had to seek to be, and have the drive to be, the heavyweight champion of the world at a time when most of white America was not particularly pleased that the strongest, most powerful man in the world was a black man. He had the opportunity, prepared for the opportunity, went for it and achieved it."

For Barrow, the link between past and present is far more than hereditary. It is etched into his being through life's lessons both learned and lived. Shortly after Joe Louis retired from the ring, he flew to New Orleans for a boxing exhibition. He was accompanied by Leonard Reed, his confidant/advisor. The two of them thought they'd get a round of golf in that morning before the exhibition, so they boarded an airport shuttle van to the hotel to drop off their baggage and race to the course. After a few minutes, Reed got off the van and asked the driver, who was standing curbside, what was the delay. The driver responded, "Mister, I can take you but I'm not allowed to take no Coloreds." Reed, a light-skinned black, turned two shades of red. "Do you know who that man is?" he asked. "That's Joe Louis." "Don't matter," said the driver. "I still can't ride no Coloreds." Louis, who had overheard the confrontation, got off the van and hailed a taxi. As the two of them started to get into the cab, the driver—a dark-skinned fellow with a thick Southern drawl—stopped them. "Sir, I don't mean no harm, but I can't ride no white man," he said. "This here cab's for Coloreds only." Reed and Louis didn't even try to explain. Louis got in the taxi; Reed hailed another one; and the two of them headed for the hotel in separate but equal modes of transportation.

One of Barrow's responsibilities in his new position is to help ensure that everyone who wants to play golf has an equal opportunity to do so. Just like his father before him, Barrow's success will be measured in the passion for the game of those he impacts. His reward, and that of those who persevered in the fight to level the lie, is realized just as much when a minority picks up a club and has a place to use it as when Tiger Woods holes a winning putt. Ultimately, America's hope is for the day when Barrow can drive past Jackson Park and any other playground where its brothers and sisters gather and notice nothing out of the ordinary. Only then will the pain from the blow to his father's body subside and the cries of his predecessors be forever muted.

A FEW SHOUTS OF JOY

The irony of a minority winning the final major championship of the century and leading golf into the new millennium might have been lost on the uninitiated. But on golf's back roads, there were more than a few shouts of joy.

My hands gripped the steering wheel a little tighter as I drove the rental car through the main entrance of Biltmore Forest Country Club. It had been nearly 30 years since I had entered those gates and never in a car but always as fast as my feet could carry me. The caddiemaster might give your bag to another caddie if you tarried. This time I came not as an eager youth in quest of some folding money but as a prematurely graying golf writer with several platinum credit cards as proof of how far I had actually traveled. Homecomings hadn't been quite the same since 1996 when my mother died. I could feel her pride, though, as I walked through the huge doors of the clubhouse. Tom Wolfe was wrong. You can go home again.

I had been in many fancy clubhouses over the years-some with much more history and tradition hanging on the walls than Biltmore Forest. Shinnecock Hills. Winged Foot. The Country Club at Brookline. Pebble Beach. Royal Troon. Pinehurst. St. Andrews. But this clubhouse was different. I half expected the bogeyman to jump from behind one of those giant columns and scare my pants off. Instead I was greeted by an elderly gentleman with a warm smile who directed me toward a small room that served as the media center that week for the U.S. Women's Amateur Championship. I had seen his bronze face many times during my caddie days, but its crow's feet were much narrower then. The welcome felt as good going down as Mama's grits.

I had returned home for what I thought would be a nice stopover on my way to Chicago and the PGA Championship, which was also being contested at Medinah CC. I soon discovered the first of three encounters with history that week awaited me on the 10th tee. There stood Dara Broadus, the most beautiful fly in the buttermilk I'd ever seen. The 20-year-old Atlantan was only the fifth African-American to qualify for the Women's Amateur and first since LaRee Pearl Sugg in 1991. It's funny but the Furman University junior didn't look out of place, although I knew she was quite possibly the first black face at BFCC with someone else carrying her clubs. She played like she belonged, too, shooting a two-day total of 152 to qualify for match play. Dara lost her first-round match, but she didn't leave Asheville empty handed. The hopes and prayers of every service person that had ever worked at Biltmore Forest went with her.

Later that week I watched from amid the dozens of well-wishers as Bill Dickey received the PGA of America's most prestigious award at Medinah. Dickey's reward for due diligence was reported nationally in newspapers and magazines, including *Minority Golf Magazine*. I also walked with Tiger to victory in the

PGA Championship, his second major championship in less than three full years on tour. Tiger would win four more PGA Tour events—eight overall—in 1999 and an unprecedented $6.6 million. He would finish the year as the undisputed number one golfer in the world. He would win his first two starts of the new millenium to run his PGA Tour win streak to six. Only Byron Nelson, winner of 11 consecutive tour events in 1945, had a longer stretch of excellence. The irony of a minority winning the final major championship of the century and leading golf into the new millenium might have been lost on the uninitiated. But on golf's back roads, there were more than a few shouts of joy.

While Tiger's dominance at the close of the century had journalists scratching their heads in disbelief, it paled in comparison to the summer madness he created in 2000. After being a prohibitive favorite and finishing a disappointing fifth at the Masters, he focused all of his energy on the season's remaining major championships. Golf's holy ground, historic Pebble Beach and the Old Course at St. Andrews in Scotland, hosted the U.S. Open and British Open, respectively. At Pebble, Tiger was solid as a rock, shooting a 12-under-par 274 to claim a third major title by a whopping 15 strokes. He shattered numerous records, including widest margin of victory in a major (Old Tom Morris won the British Open in 1862 by 13 shots) and in the U.S. Open (Willie Smith had held the previous mark at 11 strokes since 1899). "Just the perfect display of golf," said runner-up Ernie Els, himself a two-time U.S. Open champ. "If you want to watch a guy win the U.S. Open playing perfectly, you've just seen it."

Tiger was just as masterful a month later at the birthplace of golf, shooting 19-under-par 269 to win by eight shots and become, at 24 years 7 1/2 months, the youngest player to claim the career, modern Grand Slam. He joined Gene Sarazen (1935), Ben Hogan (1953), Gary Player (1965) and Jack Nicklaus (1966) as career slammers. In another record-breaking performance, Tiger again displayed precision shot-making, avoiding St. Andrews' 112 sand bunkers. He completed his summer run by successfully defending the PGA Championship at Vahalla GC in Louisville, Ky., outdueling Bob May in a scintillating playoff after setting his fourth major championship scoring record. He snared a win at the WGC-NEC Invitational at Firestone CC in Akron, Ohio, then made the Canadian Open his ninth win of the season. In Canada, he joined Lee Trevino as the only players to capture golf's Triple Crown (the U.S. Open, British Open and Canadian Open in the same year). Said Woods, "I didn't even know there was a Triple Crown until I got to Canada and everyone was talking about it."

In golfing brilliance and bravado, Tiger has evoked comparisons to Nicklaus, Hogan, Nelson, Bobby Jones and Arnold Palmer. But while he chases history in green pastures around the world, golf's brightest star hears whispers of praise from its overlooked and long forgotten lesser lights. He occasionally looks down from the mountaintop and tips his hat to those on whose shoulders he climbed to get there. To Shippen, Rhodes, Spiller, Sifford, Gregory, Gibson, Elder and all the other pioneers, we acknowledge it was a long, slow, tedious, often painful journey. But thank God, we made it.

AFRICAN-AMERICAN PGA TOUR PLAYERS

Henry Carl Baraben
Born November 18, 1933, in Jenerette, La.; turned pro in April of '58; worked in West Chester, Calif.; belonged to Southern Cal section of PGA; became member of PGA in 1968.

James W. Black
Born May 26, 1942, in Charlotte, N.C.; turned pro in 1962; joined PGA Tour in 1965 and played in 14 events, earning less than $12,000, before losing his sponsorship and dropping off the tour.

Rafe Botts
Born March 31, 1937, in Washington, D.C.; turned pro in 1960; joined PGA Tour in 1961.

Cliff Brown
Born August 10, 1929, in Birmingham, Ala.; turned pro in February of 1962 after competing in the National Public Links from 1958-61; applied for PGA of America membership Dec. 27, 1969, and became a member July 31, 1970; played in 92 PGA Tour events from 1964-69; was the head pro at Pipe O' Peace GC in Riverdale, Ill.; also owned a driving range outside Chicago.

Howard (Lefty) Brown
Born July 17, 1936, in Saginaw, Mich.; turned pro in 1960; joined the PGA Tour in 1969.

Pete Brown
Born February 2, 1935, in Port Gibson, Miss.; received Approved Tournament Player's card in 1963; won 1964 Waco Turner Open; had best year on PGA Tour in 1970 with $56,069 in official earnings (35th on money list).

Lee Carter
Born January 14, 1954, in Dallas, Texas; attended the University of New Mexico; turned pro in 1974; graduated from PGA Tour Q-school in 1979.

Gordon Chavis
Born June 29, 1938, in Bishopsville, S.C.; turned pro in 1961; joined PGA Tour in 1962.

James Lacey (Jim) Dent
Born May 9, 1939, in Augusta, Ga.; turned pro in 1966; joined PGA Tour in 1970, earning a career-best $48,486 (59th on money list) in 1974; best finish was second to Jack Nicklaus at the 1972 Walt Disney World Classic; joined Senior PGA Tour in 1989 and through 1999 he had won 12 times and earned a combined total of $7,383,082 during his career.

Lee Elder
Born July 14, 1934, in Dallas, Texas; turned pro in 1959 and joined the PGA Tour in 1967; won the 1974 Monsanto Open to become the first African-American to qualify for the Masters; also won the 1976

Houston Open, 1978 Greater Milwaukee Open and 1978 American Express Westchester Classic; amassed $1,020,514 in official PGA Tour earnings; joined the Senior PGA Tour in 1984 and won eight times, earning $1,574,222 through 1998.

Al Green
Born August 26, 1939, in Annapolis, Md.; turned pro in 1967; joined PGA Tour in 1973; teamed with Lee Elder to win the Walt Disney Team Championship in 1975.

George Johnson
Born December 8, 1938, in Columbus, Ga.; turned pro in 1964; qualified for PGA Tour in 1968; won 1971 Azalea Open and had four second-place finishes in 10-year career.

Al Morton
Joined PGA Tour in 1981; played in seven events in '82, 11 total over his career.

Charlie Owens
Born February 22, 1937, in Winter Haven, Fla.; turned pro in 1967; qualified for the PGA Tour in 1970; won the 1971 Kemper Asheville Open; earned $15,462 on the PGA Tour; joined the Senior PGA Tour in 1981; finished career-best eighth on money list (earning $207,813) in 1986, with two victories—Treasure Coast Classic and Senior Tour Roundup; made Vantage Cup Team in 1986; won Ben Hogan Award in 1987.

Calvin Peete
Born July 18, 1943, in Detroit, Mich.; turned pro in 1971; qualified for the PGA Tour in the spring of 1975; won 12 times on the PGA Tour, including 11 in the 1980s, surpassed only by Tom Kite; led the tour in driving accuracy 10 consecutive years; won the 1984 Vardon Trophy for low stroke average and played on the 1983 and 1985 Ryder Cup teams; won four times in 1982; won the 1983 Ben Hogan Award; earned $2,302,363 on PGA Tour; joined the Senior PGA Tour in 1993.

Charlie Sifford
Born June 2, 1922, in Charlotte, N.C.; turned pro in 1948; obtained Approved Tournament Player's card in 1959 and joined PGA Tour in 1960; won the 1967 Greater Hartford Open and 1969 Los Angeles Open on the PGA Tour, amassing $341,224 in career earnings; among the top-60 winners on tour from 1960-69; also won the 1957 Long Beach Open, 1963 Puerto Rico Open and 1971 Sea Pines Open; joined the Senior PGA Tour in 1980 and collected $929,502 in earnings in 19 years.

Curtis Sifford
Born May 6, 1942, in Charlotte, N.C.; turned pro in 1967; joined PGA Tour in 1969; earned career-best $21,751 in 1973.

Nathaniel Starks
Born June 20, 1940, in Brownwood, Ga.; joined PGA Tour in 1973; won $14,277 in 1974 to finish 124th on money list.

Adrian Anthony Stills
Born November 29, 1957, in Pensacola, Fla.; graduated South Carolina State University in 1979; turned pro in 1979; qualified for the PGA Tour in 1985.

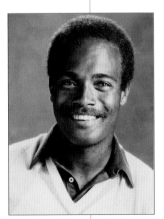

Adrian Stills

Bobby Stroble

Born December 4, 1944, in Albany, Ga.; turned pro in 1967; joined PGA Tour in 1976; tied for 30th (career-best) in the 1977 Oklahoma City Open Championship; joined the Senior PGA Tour in 1995 and earned $1,404,098 through 1999.

Ron Terry

Born July 21, 1949, in Aberdeen, Md.; graduated from Northwest Texas State University in 1971; turned pro in 1972 and joined PGA Tour in 1976.

Chuck Thorpe

Born January 22, 1947, in Roxboro, N.C.; turned pro in 1967; joined PGA Tour in 1972 and tied for 10th in the Houston Open in 1973.

Jimmy Lee (Jim) Thorpe

Born February 1, 1949, in Roxboro, N.C.; turned pro in 1972; joined PGA Tour in 1976; won the 1985 Greater Milwaukee Open, 1985 and 1986 Seiko Tucson Match Play Championships; earned $1,935,566 on PGA Tour; joined the Senior PGA Tour in 1999.

James (Junior) Walker Jr.

Born November 26, 1938, in Rocky Mountain, N.C.; joined the PGA Tour in 1965; best finish tie for 30th in Westchester Open in 1965 and L.A. Open in 1969; regained tour card at '68 qualifying tournament.

Tom Woodard

Born December 2, 1955, in Midland, Texas; turned pro in 1978; joined PGA Tour in 1981; regained tour card at '84 qualifying tournament.

William (Bill) Wright

Born April 4, 1936, in Kansas City, Mo.; won the National Public Links championship in 1959 and NAIA individual crown in 1960; turned pro in 1964 and joined the PGA Tour that year.

Pete Brown and Charlie Sifford said the following players had tour cards but these could not be confirmed:

Willie Brown

of Houston

Dick Thomas

of Baltimore

Excellent players who had enough game to play on the PGA Tour but for one reason or another never did:

Jesse Allen of Jackson, Miss.; **William (Bill) Bishop** of Philadelphia, Pa.; **Butch Bowers** of Nashville, Ill.; **Moses Brooks** of Dallas, Texas.; **(Cross-handed) Henry Brown** of Augusta, Ga.; **Fred Carter** of Dallas, Texas.; **Joe (Roach) Delancey** of Miami, Fla.; **Herman DuBois**, of New York City, N.Y.; **Reginald Golden** of Houston, Texas.; **Gordon Goodson** of Baltimore, Md.; **Olin Grant** of Charleston, S.C.; **Alvin Greer**; **Douglas Greer**; **Joe Hampton** of Hartford, Conn.; **Harry Jeter** of Asheville, N.C.; **Leonard Jones** of Dallas, Texas; **Bobby Mays** of Philadelphia, Pa.; **Paul Reed** of Galveston, Texas; **Martin Roach** of Orangeburg, S.C.; **Carl Seldon** of Atlanta; **Calvin Tanner** of Chicago, Ill.; **Bill Thorpe** of Roxboro, N.C.; **Robert Walker** of Thomaston, Ga.; **Jimmy Wesley** of Savannah, Ga.; **J.W. White** of Dallas, Texas; **Jimmy Woods** of Cincinnati, Ohio.

Note: *The Ladies Professional Golf Association Tour had only three African-American members —* **Althea Gibson**, **Renee Powell** *and* **LaRee Pearl Sugg**.